The Rules in Practice

Revised Fourth Edition

D1253953

Free Update Service

The Racing Rules of Sailing (1997–2000) are very different from the pre-1997 rules.
In their first few years of use there may be changes and developments, and new interpretations.

If you would like a free update, send an SAE to
Fernhurst Books, Duke's Path, High Street, Arundel, West Sussex, BN18 9AJ.
or
East Shore Sailing, 1000 East Shore Drive, Ithaca, NY 14850, USA.
or
dial our Web site http://fernhurst.com

The Rules in Practice

Bryan Willis

First published 1997 by Fernhurst Books,
Duke's Path, High Street, Arundel, West Sussex,
BN18 9AJ, UK.
Tel: 01903 882277 Fax: 01903 882715
**Write, phone or fax the publisher
for a free, full-colour brochure.**

Printed and bound in Great Britain

British Library Cataloguing in Publication Data:
A catalogue record for this book is available
from the British Library.
ISBN 1 898660 33 6

This fourth edition has been completely re-
written in line with the new rules, approved at
the International Sailing Federation conference
in November 1996, and becoming effective in
April 1997.

Cover design by Simon Balley

Cover photograph by Peter Bentley

Design and DTP by Creative Byte of Poole

Drawings from photos by Shelley Baxter

Edited by Tim Davison

Printed by Hillman Printers, Frome

Contents

Introduction 6

The Rule Changes 7

1   The Basics 9

2   Before the Preparatory Signal 15

3   In the Preparatory Period 16

4   The Start 21

5   The Gate Start 28

6   On the Beat 29

7   Rounding the Windward Mark 38

8   On the Reach 49

9   Rounding the Wing Mark 57

10 Rounding the Leeward Mark from the Reach 62

11 On the Run 64

12 Rounding the Leeward Mark from the Run 70

13 The Finish 74

14 Means of Propulsion 77

15 Taking a Penalty 78

16 Protesting 80

17 Requesting Redress & Appealing 83

The 1997–2000 Rules and selected Appendices: 85

Sportsmanship and the Rules 85

Introduction 85

Part 1 Fundamental Rules 85

Part 2 When Boats Meet 85

Part 3 Conduct of a Race 86

Part 4 Other Requirements When Racing 87

Part 5 Protests, Hearings, Misconduct and Appeals 88

Part 6 Entry and Qualification 90

Part 7 Race Organization 91

Appendices

A Scoring 91

G Advertising 92

J Weighing Clothing and Equipment 93

K Competitors' ISAF Eligibility 93

L Banned Substances and Banned Methods 94

Definitions 95

Introduction

This book is primarily for competitive sailors who race in dinghies and keelboats. The Racing Rules of Sailing apply to all forms of sailboat racing, though there are some variations for sailboards, match racing, and team racing. I have aimed to examine about one hundred situations which are a regular feature of both championship and club racing. Unlike most other books on the racing rules, I look at these situations from the point of view of you, the helmsman. Placing you in each of the boats involved in turn, I explain your rights and your obligations. Being confident about this knowledge not only means you avoid breaking a rule and have to take a penalty, but that you can concentrate on exploiting the situation to gain boat lengths over your immediate rivals.

It is popular misconception that to be good at boat-to-boat tactics you need to know the rules. The rules, the rule numbers, the case law; all that can be sorted out before the start of the hearing if there is a protest. What you need to know out there on the water are your rights and your obligations; what you are allowed to do, and what you must and mustn't do. You need to know them automatically and subconsciously, so that you can concentrate on manoeuvring and sailing fast, to exploit the situation to the full. It is just as satisfying to come away from a mark in the lead having approached it in second place as it is to spend twenty minutes overhauling your rival with superior boatspeed. There is no satisfaction in sailing faster than everyone else on a leg if you throw away your position through being uncertain about your rights and obligations when you come to round the mark.

The book should also be useful in the preparation of protests. Each situation shows the critical questions which have to be considered and which will determine the 'facts found' - and, therefore, the result of the hearing.

Because almost all the rules of racing apply to the boats rather than to the people sailing them, most books on the rules, and indeed the rules themselves, use the pronoun 'she'. Since I aim to look at situations from the point of view of you, the helmsman, I use the pronoun 'you'; and for the helmsman of the other boat 'he' and 'him'*. However, bear in mind that it is what the boat does that matters. The intentions of the people sailing the boats are irrelevant (provided that they are not malicious). Even most hails are irrelevant. What each boat actually does is usually all that counts.

This fourth edition has been updated to comply with the major changes introduced in 1997 by the ISAF, (the International Sailing Federation, formerly the International Yacht Racing Union).

* Publisher's note: 'or she' is implied throughout.

The Rule Changes

Every four years the rules are updated. You may have heard that the new 'Racing Rules of Sailing' (1997-2000) are dramatically different from the 'Yacht Racing Rules' (1992-96). In fact although they have been completely re-written into a more modern simplified form, the new rules change the game very little. Certainly, sailors who fleet race and care most about boatspeed rather than boat-to-boat tactics will find their game not changed very much.

I am going to describe here the most significant changes. If you are learning the rules for the first time, or paid little attention to them till now, you should not bother with how things were. This chapter is not for you!

If you've been racing for a while but don't take racing too seriously you should read just the first part. Experienced competitors who use the rules tactically (and that includes everyone who team races or match races), will discover there are some important changes and will want to read this whole chapter.

I will not include changes which are for simplification, only those which 'change the game'.

The changes almost all sailors need to know

Under the old rules, after starting and clearing the starting line, a leeward boat with luffing rights could 'luff as she pleased', meaning she could luff without giving the windward boat any chance to keep clear. Under the new rules, any right-of-way boat that changes course must give the other boat room to keep clear. This change removes the anomaly of having a rule that allowed, indeed encouraged, collisions, although they rarely resulted in damage.

There is no longer the complicated relationship of 'mast-abeam' between a windward boat and a leeward boat. So when a leeward boat is luffing, the windward boat cannot claim she is 'mast-abeam' to stop the luff and make the leeward boat return to her proper course. The leeward boat can keep luffing, but always giving room to the windward boat to keep clear.

The 720 degree turns penalty is now standard, so if the sailing instructions make no other provision, the 720 degree penalty system applies.

Changes affecting more experienced sailors

For many sailors, the changes above are all they need to know. The next group of changes will interest those who use boat-to-boat tactics in fleet racing, and especially those who team and match race.

The old rules allowed a right-of-way boat to make contact with another boat, even if damage resulted. Only if there was 'serious damage' could the right-of-way boat be penalised. Now, every boat must avoid contact with another boat if reasonably possible. However a right-of-way boat (or one entitled to room) need not act to avoid contact until it is clear that the other boat is not keeping clear (or giving room), and will not be penalised unless there is contact that causes damage. A boat that breaks the rule may take a 720 degree penalty provided the damage is not serious. A give-way boat (or a boat required to give room) that breaks this rule and a 'when boats meet' rule, may exonerate herself by taking just one 720 degree penalty.

Unlike the old Rule 35 that it replaces, the new Rule 16 (that says a right-of-way boat changing course must give the other boat room to keep clear) has no exceptions. So even when a boat is 'assuming a proper course when rounding a mark', or when a starboard-tack boat is luffing up to close-hauled near a port-tack boat after the starting signal, the right-of-way boat must give room for the other boat to keep clear.

Under the old rules, whether or not a leeward boat had 'luffing rights' (the right to sail above close-hauled) before the start depended on their relative positions. Whether a leeward boat had luffing rights after the start depended on the relationship when the leeward boat started. Now, before or after the start, a leeward boat always has luffing rights unless she established the overlap from clear astern within two boat-lengths (laterally) of the windward boat.

However, as there is no proper course before the start, when a boat gets an overlap to leeward, having 'initially given the other boat room to keep clear' the leeward boat may luff up to head to wind while maintaining a small overlap, whereas she used to have to stop at close-hauled while the windward boat was ahead of mast-abeam.

A close-hauled port-tack boat approaching a port-hand windward mark close to the layline (hoping to tack just ahead of a starboard-tack boat approaching on the starboard layline) will find the new rules stacked against her. If she completes her tack onto starboard within the 'two-boat-circle', she must give the starboard-tack boat room to round the mark even if she completes the tack clear ahead.

An inside leeward boat with luffing rights must gybe at a mark where her proper course requires a gybe, whereas she used to be able to sail the windward boat on or luff at any time before or during the rounding.

When on a leg other than a windward leg, the old rules and the new rules say that a boat may not sail below her proper course when there is a boat to leeward or astern steering a course to leeward. The old rule applied when the boats were within three lengths; the new rules change this to two lengths. So 'two lengths' becomes the standard distance for everything except the distance used in the definition of 'obstruction' which remains at one-length.

The old rules were not clear about the rights and obligations when a boat was sailing backwards when manoeuvring for position at the start. There is now a rule that says a boat moving astern by backing a sail must keep clear of one that is not.

There is no longer an onus on a tacking boat to

satisfy the protest committee that she tacked in time, but a boat doing a 'slam-dunk' (crossing ahead and completing a tack on the other boat's weather bow) cannot claim 'mast-abeam' to remove the leeward boat's luffing rights because there is no longer a 'mast-abeam' position. If the leeward boat is overlapped as the tacking boat passes through head-to-wind, the leeward boat may sail above her proper (close-hauled) course (provided she gives room to the tacking boat to keep clear).

Class rules may no longer over-rule the prohibition on weight jackets, and the total permitted weight for clothing has been lowered from 15 to 8 kilograms, but this does not include a harness or footwear, and can be varied within certain limits by class rules.

There is no longer a rule requiring at least one of the two boats involved in a collision (other than a minor and unavoidable collision) to retire, take a penalty, or protest. So now when two boats collide and the right-of-way boat could not have avoided contact (or if there is no damage), and the give-way boat does not protest, retire, or take a penalty, then the right-of-way boat cannot be penalised if she sails on without protesting. A third yacht could, and still can, successfully protest the give-way boat, but no longer both boats. There is no longer any reference to 'minor and unavoidable' collisions.

Singlehanders who protest will now have to keep their protest flag displayed permanently as there is no longer any dispensation. The hail of 'protest' can now be made 'at the first reasonable opportunity' rather than 'immediately', but the actual word 'protest' must be used. Any red flag conspicuously displayed will now qualify as a protest flag. A protesting boat wanting to withdraw her protest may now do so 'if approved by the protest committee'.

The new rules make clear that a 'warning' given to a competitor for a gross breach of sportsmanship is not a 'penalty'. As the competitor's national authority must still be informed only when a penalty is imposed, the procedure might be more readily used when a 'breach of good sportsmanship' is suspected.

1 The Basics

There are certain obligations which you have all the time, so I will state them here and not repeat them in the rest of the book.

You must sail fairly. Sailboat racing is the greatest sport. Generally, we don't have umpires or judges or referees; we police ourselves. Cheats can spoil any sport, and currently our sport is free of cheats (unlike many other sports). We all need to work to keep it that way. So the rules require that you conduct yourself in a sportsmanlike manner at all times, and don't bring the sport into disrepute. This principle applies as much to club racing as it does to championships. Trying to gain an advantage by deliberately infringing a rule or lying at a protest hearing is nothing less than cheating and the penalties for cheating can be severe. In recent years, competitors found guilty of cheating have been disqualified from entire championships and some have been banned by their national authorities from taking part in competitive sailing for a year or more (Rules: 'Sportsmanship' & 69 'Allegations of Gross Misconduct').

You must help anyone you see in danger. If you lose a position while acting the hero, you may be entitled to redress. (Rule 1 'Helping those in danger').

When you have infringed a rule, you must promptly do your penalty turns. To continue to race without taking a penalty knowing you have infringed a rule and gained an advantage, hoping perhaps that no one will protest, or through your courtroom skills you might outwit a protestor in the protest room, is an infringement of the fundamental non-numbered rule about 'Sportsmanship'.

Even when you have right-of-way or the right to room, you must try to avoid contact. If you don't, and there is damage, you may be disqualified after a protest hearing (Rule 14 'Avoiding Contact').

Unless you are racing in a category of event which allows advertising, you must not 'advertise' on your hull, or crew or equipment during a regatta, even when you're not racing. (Rule 79 'Advertising').

I emphasise that these principles apply all the time, and to every situation described in this book.

There are a few terms and definitions which you need to know before we start.

International Sailing Federation (ISAF)

(The A in ISAF is there because the International Softball Federation bagged the initials ISF before the ISAF changed its name in September 1996 from the International Yacht Racing Union): The international governing body which produces the racing rules and, for guidance on their interpretation, publishes cases which have been decided and submitted by national authorities.

Organising authority

The body which decides to hold an event and arranges the venue. The organising authority might be a club, a class association or a national authority, or a combination of these. It must appoint a race committee. At a principal event (such as an open regatta or a national championship) it may also appoint a jury, or at an international event, an international jury.

Race committee

The race committee is responsible for producing sailing instructions, organising the racing and publishing the results. When no jury or international jury has been appointed, the race committee must appoint a protest committee if one is needed.

Protest committee

A protest committee is appointed by the race committee when neither a jury nor an international jury has been appointed by the organising authority, to hear protests and requests for redress. The term 'protest committee' is also used to describe a jury or international jury when it hears protests and requests for redress.

Jury

A committee separate from and independent of the race committee, appointed by the organising authority at a major event. In addition to hearing protests and requests for redress, its members often go afloat during racing to encourage rule compliance (in particular with Rule 42 'Propulsion').

International jury

Appointed by the organising authority, its role is the same as that of a jury. However, its membership is made up of people of different nationalities, some of whom must be international judges (appointed by the ISAF). Provided that it conducts itself in accordance with the procedures described in Appendix Q, its decisions are not open to appeal.

Appeal authority

Each national authority appoints a committee to hear appeals by competitors against decisions of protest committees and juries (but not International Juries). For example, in the United Kingdom, the Royal Yachting Association's Racing Rules Committee hears appeals; in the United States of America, appeals are decided by District Appeals Committees, and some are subsequently referred to the United States Sailing Association's Appeals Committee.

Obstruction

'An obstruction is an object that a boat could not pass without changing course substantially, if she were sailing directly towards it and one of her hull lengths from it. An object that can be safely passed on only one side and an area so designated by the sailing instructions are also obstructions. However, a boat *keeping clear* or *giving room* to other boats when so required is not an obstruction to them.' The committee boat, a rescue boat, a capsized dinghy, the shore, perceived underwater dangers or shallows, and a boat on starboard-tack on a collision course in relation to a port-tack boat are all obstructions. In the case of the committee boat it will also be a mark when it is specified as being at one end of the starting or finish line. A half-metre diameter inflatable buoy is not an obstruction.

Keeping clear (see diagram opposite)

'One boat keeps clear of another if the other can sail her course with no need to take avoiding action and, when the boats are overlapped on the same tack, if the leeward boat could change course without immediately making contact with the windward boat.' In dinghies in a Force 2 on flat water, 'keeping clear' can be synonymous with 'avoiding a collision' (for example in a 'port and starboard' encounter on a beat in which the port-tack boat ducks under the stern of the starboard-tack boat), but were they to be large keelboats in a Force 6 and a heavy sea, an obligation on you to 'keep clear' might mean leaving a boat-length or more between you and the right-of-way boat. Furthermore, when you are the give-way boat, you must not intimidate the right-of-way boat such that he thinks there is going to be a collision and is forced to take avoiding action. So even in fairly light conditions it's as well to give him a smile, so he knows you are paying attention, before diving under his stern and missing him by a millimetre.

Hailing

A hail is a meaningful word or string of words capable of being heard in the prevailing conditions by the occupants of the boat to which it is addressed. (This is not a defined term in the rule book - but it's a useful definition, supported by appeal cases.)

You are never actually **required** to make a hail, but when you want to protest you have to hail "protest" at the first reasonable opportunity; and when you want a boat to give you room to tack, when you're approaching an obstruction close-hauled, he is not required to take any action until you hail.

When the other boat hails you, you don't always have to respond. You should remember the situations when you must respond to a hail from the other boat:

•   When he hails for room to tack because he's close-hauled approaching an obstruction.

•   When, after you have hailed for water to tack because you are close-hauled and need room to tack at an obstruction, he replies "you tack".

Some other hails might help to establish something, such as the right to room at a mark, or warn a port-tack boat of your presence

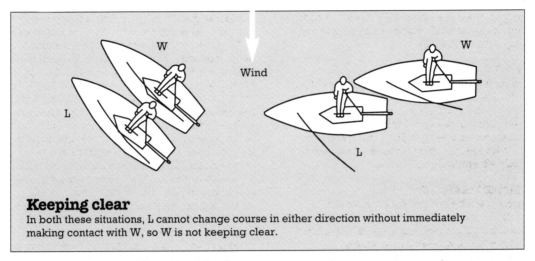

Keeping clear
In both these situations, L cannot change course in either direction without immediately making contact with W, so W is not keeping clear.

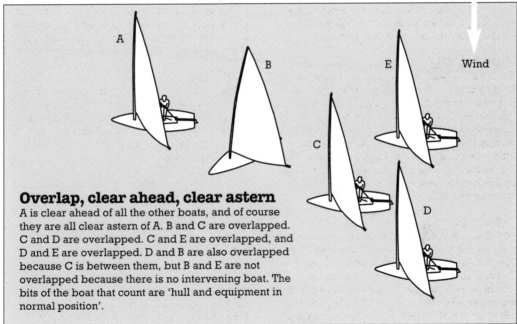

Overlap, clear ahead, clear astern
A is clear ahead of all the other boats, and of course they are all clear astern of A. B and C are overlapped. C and D are overlapped. C and E are overlapped, and D and E are overlapped. D and B are also overlapped because C is between them, but B and E are not overlapped because there is no intervening boat. The bits of the boat that count are 'hull and equipment in normal position'.

("Starboard!") but these hails in themselves place no obligation on anyone to do anything.

When a hail from you means the other boat must respond, there is the obvious obligation on you not to make the hail unless you have the right to do so. For example, when you are close-hauled and believe you are approaching shallow water and cannot tack without the possibility of colliding with a boat astern or to windward, you may of course hail for room to tack, but you have no right to hail merely for tactical reasons.

Layline
The course (over the ground) on which your boat, sailing close-hauled on starboard tack, can just lay a windward mark which is to be rounded to port is the starboard-tack layline for that mark, and the most windward line on which you would approach the mark on port tack is the port-tack layline. High performance boats with spinnakers or large headsails go faster down-wind by reaching and gybing, so a leeward mark has laylines which are the proper courses for the boats approaching on each tack. Tidal

streams distort laylines; a stream going with the wind makes the angle between the windward mark port and starboard laylines wider, and the leeward mark laylines narrower. As the wind gets lighter, the angle between the leeward mark laylines for high-performance boats with powerful spinnakers or genikers gets dramatically wider. A cross-course tidal stream swings the laylines towards the tide. 'Layline' is not a term used in the rule book, but the term 'proper course' is, and laylines are the extremes of proper courses, so need to be understood. And to be a good tactician an understanding of laylines is essential.

Luffing rights

This term is not used in the rule book either, but it is often used by sailors, and so I use it in this book. You have 'luffing rights' when you have the right to sail higher than your proper course, forcing a boat to windward of you to alter course to keep clear. Provided you didn't establish the overlap to leeward of the windward boat, from astern and within two lengths, a leeward boat has luffing rights after the start, and may luff right up to head-to-wind, but she must give the windward boat room to keep clear. (Rule 11)

Before the starting signal, because there is no 'proper course', any leeward boat may luff up to head-to-wind no matter how the overlap was established (provided the windward boat can keep clear), but at the moment the starting signal is made, any leeward boat that established the overlap from clear astern must bear away to close-hauled (if the first leg is a beat) unless as a result of sailing above close-hauled she becomes clear astern (which allows her to tack out of the windward boat's wind-shadow). (Rule 17.1)

Proper course (see diagram opposite)

A proper course is ' A course a boat would sail to finish as soon as possible in the absence of the other boats referred to in the rule using the term. A boat has no proper course before her starting signal.' You're never required to sail a proper course, but there are some situations in which you mustn't sail above your proper course, and others in which you mustn't sail below your proper course, so you need to know what a proper course is.

Sailing instructions

The race committee must produce sailing instructions and make them available to you in time for you to read them before the race or series. They contain two types of information:

* The intentions of the race committee; these instructions contain the word 'will'. For example, 'All marks will be large orange spheres'.

* The obligations of the individual competitors and the competing boats; these instruction contain the word 'shall'. For example, 'All marks shall be rounded to port'.

The two types of instructions are usually mixed together because they are ordered chronologically.

It is imperative that the sailing instructions are studied carefully before a race or series. I doubt if there is a single champion who has not at some time lost an important race or series through failing to read or remember some particular sailing instruction.

The penalty for not complying with a sailing instruction describing an obligation of a boat is disqualification from a race (unless some other penalty is specified), but the penalty can usually be applied only after a hearing.

No such penalty can be applied to the race committee when it does not carry out its own intentions specified in the sailing instructions, or it fails to comply with a rule which governs its conduct (Parts 3 and 7 of the rules). What penalty could be imposed without adversely affecting innocent competitors? (Yes, of course the committee could be hung, drawn and quartered, but who would run the next race?) You should bear in mind that the race committee is invariably trying to do a good job of running the races. If the committee makes an error or an omission and this affects your finishing position in the race or series, (and *only* if it affects your finishing position), then you can ask for 'redress'. A good race committee that realises its action has affected a boat's finishing position, will itself initiate a redress hearing. Chapter 18 deals with redress hearings. The most common error is to write confusing or ambiguous sailing instructions about the course, resulting in some boats sailing one course and some sailing another.

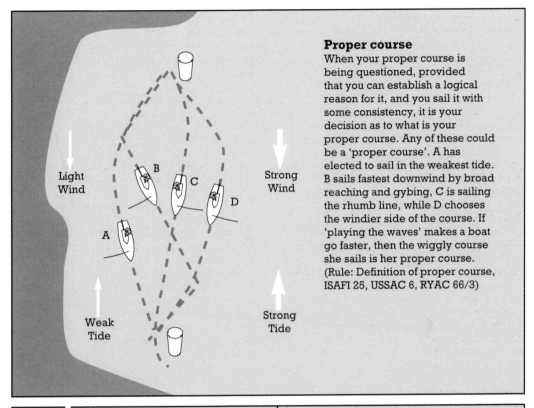

Proper course

When your proper course is being questioned, provided that you can establish a logical reason for it, and you sail it with some consistency, it is your decision as to what is your proper course. Any of these could be a 'proper course'. A has elected to sail in the weakest tide. B sails fastest downwind by broad reaching and gybing, C is sailing the rhumb line, while D chooses the windier side of the course. If 'playing the waves' makes a boat go faster, then the wiggly course she sails is her proper course. (Rule: Definition of proper course, ISAFI 25, USSAC 6, RYAC 66/3)

Sailing the course

For this triangular course the sailing instructions read 'Course: mark A, round to port; mark B, round to port; mark C round to port, finish'. In this case it's OK to leave mark B to starboard (or to collide with it) on the way from the start to mark A, because mark B is not a mark that 'begins, bounds or ends' the first leg. (Rule 31.1)

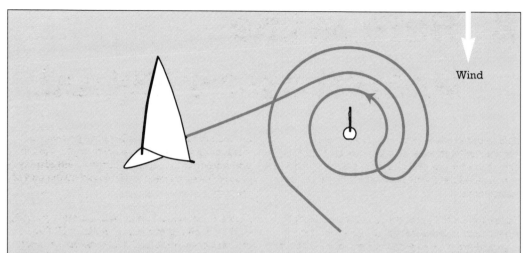

If you leave a mark which does 'begin, bound or end a leg' on which you're sailing, on the wrong side, you can go back and 'unwind' but make sure that the net result is that you have actually rounded the mark and not left it out altogether. This is called 'the string test'. (This diagram shows a corrected course.) (Rule 29.1)

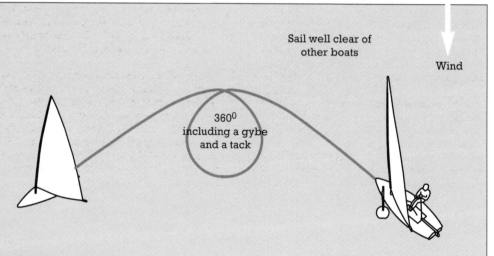

Sail well clear of other boats

Wind

360° including a gybe and a tack

Touching a mark:

If you touch a starting mark after the preparatory signal, or a mark which 'begins, bounds or ends' the leg on which you're sailing, or a finishing mark before you have finished and cleared the line and marks, you may exonerate yourself by getting well clear of all other boats as soon as possible and immediately completing a 360° circle including a tack and a gybe. (Rule 31.2).

2 Before the Preparatory Signal

Before going afloat you will have to enter, register or 'sign on' and may be required to show your measurement certificate. These requirements will be specified in the sailing instructions.

To the water! Although the 'when boats meet' rules apply to boats before the preparatory signal, there is no *penalty* for infringing a 'when boats meet' rule unless you interfere with a boat that is racing. (Rule 22.1)

Rules or sailing instructions (including all of Part 4 of the rules) requiring you to do something 'whilst racing' don't apply either, because you're not racing till the preparatory signal.

However, you can be disqualified (after a protest and a hearing) for infringing some other sailing instruction, even if you're not racing when the infringement occurs, and if you're in the wrong in an incident where there was damage, you could be liable for the damage.

If your boat is damaged in a collision and it wasn't your fault, it is useful to have a protest form showing that the hearing found the other person was in the wrong. So it's worth remembering that you can protest another boat for breaking a rule of Part 2 (the 'when boats meet' rules) before the preparatory signal, and

the race committee must hear the protest if it is valid, even though no penalty is applied to the other boat. You must hail "Protest" and display a protest flag, and keep it displayed till the end of the race.

Before every start there is a preparatory period, the beginning of which is signalled with the preparatory signal. But before the preparatory signal there is a warning signal (usually your class flag or a yellow shape, displayed ten minutes before the start, accompanied by a sound signal) the purpose of which is simply to warn you that in so many minutes (usually five) the preparatory signal will be made. The preparatory signal (usually code flap 'P' or a blue shape, displayed five minutes before the starting signal, accompanied by a sound signal) means that boats are now *'racing'* (even though they are not going anywhere!) and gives an accurate time warning so that you know exactly when the starting signal will be made.

You should be near the committee boat and watching it closely when the preparatory signal is made so that you can set your watch. This is especially important in a big fleet where you might start some distance from the committee boat and it is often impossible to see the visual starting signal or hear the 'gun' (and remember, the sound takes several seconds to travel the length of a long starting line).

3 In the Preparatory Period

This section covers the period from the preparatory signal to the time at which boats are approaching the line to start.

At the moment of the preparatory signal you must be afloat and off moorings and thereafter not be hauled out or 'made fast' (tied up) except to bail or reef or make repairs. However, you may anchor at any time, but you must recover your anchor if possible before proceeding. Your crew may stand on the bottom (in shallow water of course), to hold the boat. (Rule 45)

You are vulnerable in the preparatory period because no-one is sailing any particular course and the risk of collision is great. However, if you infringe a rule of Part 2 (the 'when boats meet' rules) you can take a penalty (by getting well clear of other boats and 'doing a 720') as soon as possible after the incident, so unless the infringement is shortly before the starting signal, the penalty is a light one. (Rule 44.1)

If you hit a starting mark, you may exonerate yourself by getting well clear of other boats as soon as possible and 'doing a 360'. (Rule 31.2)

If you are going to sail in championships or open regattas, you need to know the starting penalty signals and systems because they may affect the way you plan your start (balancing the risk of being premature and the reward of getting a cracking good start):

No penalty

The vast majority of races are started with no penalty system in force. You are allowed to be on the course side of the starting line right up to the starting signal. If you are on the wrong side of the line at the moment of the start, you simply have to get back completely behind the line to start properly. On a starting line with plenty of room, the cost of making a mistake (by crossing prematurely) is small.

The I flag ('Round the ends')

When an I flag is displayed with the preparatory signal, the 'round the ends' rule will come into effect one minute before the starting signal. This means that in the final minute, if any part of your boat is on the wrong side of the line, you must return to the pre-start side round one of the ends of the line. The race committee has no obligation to tell the boats that are required to go round an end, and at major championships it never does. You'll have to make up your own mind. The idea of the rule is that it stops boats milling around on the course side of the line in the final minute, and encourages boats not to start prematurely, especially in the middle of the starting line.

The Z flag (20% penalty)

When a Z flag is displayed with the preparatory signal, if any part of your boat is on the wrong side of the line in the final minute and there is a 'general recall' you will get a 20% penalty for that race. That means that when the race does get going, your finishing position will have 20% of the number of boats entered for the race added on. If on the other hand there is no general recall then you'll be scored as a premature starter, unless you go back and restart properly, but you don't have to sail back round an end.

The black flag (disqualification)

When a black flag is displayed with the preparatory signal, and in the final minute any part of your boat is on the wrong side of the line, you will be disqualified, whether or not there is a 'general recall'. If there is a general recall you must sail home. Even if the race doesn't get started that day, you won't be eligible to start in it when it does get started.

These 'starting penalty' systems can be brought into force for any start. The race committee simply displays the appropriate flag with the preparatory signal.

Now to the boat-to-boat situations......

You are A:
• You're on port tack (because your sail is on the starboard side) so you're the give-way boat and you must keep clear. (Rule 10)
• If you alter course so that you are no longer on a collision course, and B alters course back onto a collision course, you must alter course again and make every effort to keep clear. (Rule 10)

You are B:
• You're the right-of-way boat.
• You may change course, but if you do you must give A room to keep clear, so you mustn't change course so close to A so as to prevent him from keeping clear, or make it difficult for him to keep clear. At a protest hearing, if there is a collision and doubt whether in altering course close to A you obstructed him, a protest committee is likely to find against you. (Rule 16)

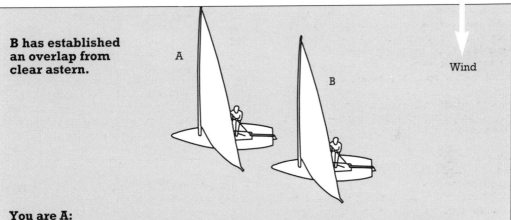

B has established an overlap from clear astern.

You are A:
• While there's no overlap, you may alter course as you please; you have no obligations.
• When B gets his overlap to leeward, the situation changes and you must now keep clear of him.
• You need do nothing till there's an overlap, even if you are sitting 'hove-to'; but once he's established the overlap you must manoeuvre to keep clear (by luffing or drawing ahead or even tacking if need be). Bear in mind once he's given you a chance to keep clear, he's is allowed to luff right up to head-to-wind. (Rule 11)

You are B:
• While you are clear astern you must keep clear. (Rule 12)
• You mustn't establish an overlap so close to A that if A luffed or bore away he would immediately make contact (Rules 11, Definition of 'keep clear', 64.1(a))
• Once you are overlapped, you become the right-of-way boat and may luff right up to head-to-wind. However, you must give A room to keep clear. Even if you don't luff, you can't come charging in while A is hove-to and not give him room to pull his sail in and get going. (Rules 11, 15, 16)

**B establishes an overlap
to windward of A.**

Wind

You are A:
• Before the overlap you have no obligations, except that any change of course must be such that it gives B room to keep clear. (Rules 12 & 16)

• When B gets an overlap nothing changes; you may still alter course if you wish and you must give B room to keep clear. (Rules 11 & 16)

• You may continue to luff, up to-head-wind, provided that B is given room to keep clear. (Rules 11 & 16)

• However, if there is an obstruction (such as the committee boat) to windward of B which prevents B from responding, then you may not luff; indeed you may even have to bear away to give B room to pass the obstruction. (Rules 18.1, 18.2(a))

You are B:
• You must keep clear before and after you are overlapped. (Rules 12 & 11)

The general principle about windward and leeward situations in the preparatory period is that a leeward boat may luff up to head-to-wind provided it gives the windward boat room to keep clear. It doesn't matter how the overlap was established, or the relative positions fore-and-aft of the two boats. The windward boat must keep clear.

A and B are overlapped approaching an obstruction, (which may or may not be a mark) before they are approaching the line to start.

You are A: You must keep clear, but if B decides to go under the committee boat, you have the right to room if you want to do the same.

Your are B: You may choose to go either to windward or to leeward of the committee boat, in spite of any protestations from A. But if you decide to go to windward, you must change course in such a way that A is able to keep clear. If you go to leeward you must give A room to pass under the committee boat if he wants to.

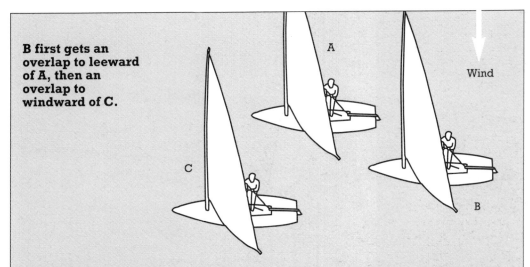

B first gets an overlap to leeward of A, then an overlap to windward of C.

Wind

You are A: When B first gets an overlap to leeward of you, because there is a possibility of his bow running into your boom, you must begin to manoeuvre to keep clear. If B luffs after he gets the overlap, you will have to luff too. If B is sailing higher than you are, you'll have to luff, but you don't have to begin to do anything until there is an overlap. (Rule 11)

You are B: When you're astern, you must keep clear. When you first get the overlap to leeward of A, it must not be so close that if A luffs there will be contact. You must give A room to keep clear. Provided you give room, you may luff. You must keep clear of C even if he luffs. If there is not enough room between A and C for you to get between them when you first get your overlap to windward of C, then you don't have the right to go in there. C has the right to luff, and if he chooses to luff the gap will get smaller, so you are in a pretty precarious position! (Rules 12 & 11 & Definition of 'Keep Clear')

You are C: You may luff if you wish, but if you do you must allow B and A room to keep clear. (Rule 16)

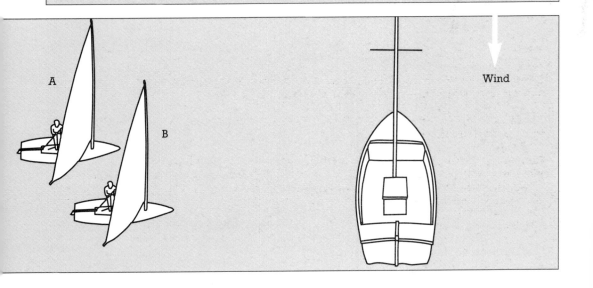

Wind

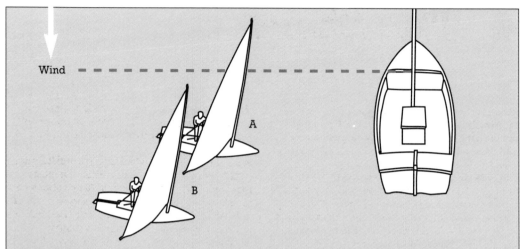

Wind

A

B

You are A: You have the right to room to pass under the committee boat even though it's a starting mark because you are not 'approaching the line to start'. You don't have to hail, but it's probably a good idea if you think you're not being given enough room. You can change your mind and tack if you want to.

You are B: It is too late now to decide to go to windward of the committee boat, so you must give room to A whether he asks for it or not. You need to give sufficient room for A to pass 'in a seamanlike way'. (Rule 18.2(a))

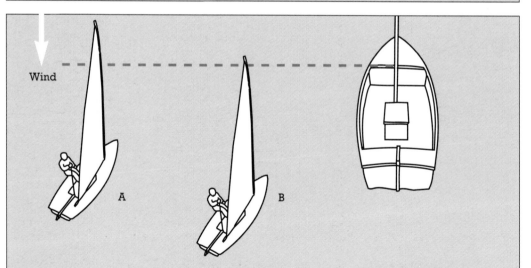

Wind

A

B

You are A: You are the give-way boat and if B luffs you must keep clear, but if B tacks you become the right-of-way boat while he's tacking and B must keep clear of you. (Rule 11)

You are B: You have no right to hail for room to tack (whether or not you are approaching the starting line to start) because the committee boat is a starting mark and the rules don't give you the right to room to tack at a starting mark if it's surrounded by navigable water. You had better bear away before you get trapped. If there is any boats to leeward of you they must give you room to pass under the committee boat. (Rule 13)

4 The Start

This section covers the period from your approach to the starting line shortly before the starting signal, to when you have started and cleared the starting line.

The race committee must make the time between the preparatory signal and the starting signal exactly correct, and must make the correct visual signals at those times. It is allowed to fail to make the sound signal, but the visual signals must be on time. That is why it is important that you check the preparatory signal by watching the committee boat signals (or better still, listening to the time-keeper counting down to the preparatory signal, if you can get close enough); then you can rely on the starting signal being exactly five minutes later. (Rule 26)

When the race committee makes a recall signal (when there are premature starters), it must make not only the visual signal (flag X) but also the sound signal (an additional bang or horn). If it doesn't, and you are in doubt as to whether or not you are a premature starter, you may assume you have started correctly and sail on. If you are in no doubt that you are a premature starter, you must return to start properly. (Rule 29.1, ISAF Case 70)

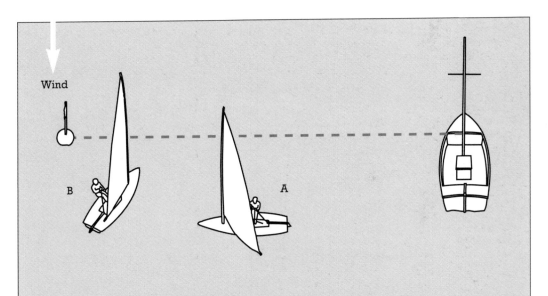

Figure 1 shows the position at the moment of the starting signal.

You are A: You may want to luff to close-hauled but you may not. B is keeping clear and to luff now would deprive him of room to keep clear. (Rule 16)

You are B: You are the give-way boat, but your course and speed will mean you will pass safely ahead of A who is not allowed to alter course to obstruct you. Mind you, if there is an incident and he didn't luff, you'll be likely to lose the protest!

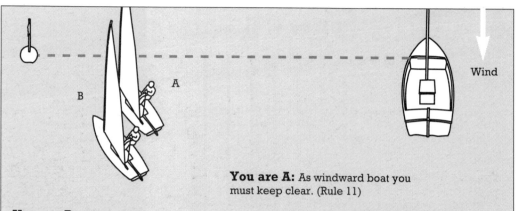

You are A: As windward boat you must keep clear. (Rule 11)

You are B: However you came to be overlapped to leeward, (you might have come from astern, or you might have tacked to leeward of A), and whether or not the starting gun has gone, you may luff (above close-hauled if necessary) to get round the mark, but you must give A room to keep clear. If you established the overlap from clear astern, then you mustn't sail above your proper course, so once you have passed the mark you must bear away to close-hauled or below.

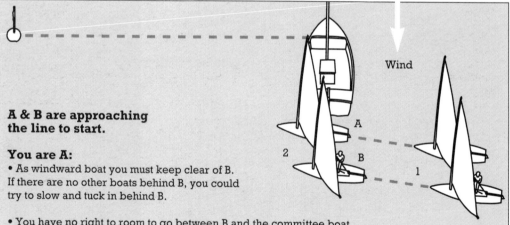

A & B are approaching the line to start.

You are A:
• As windward boat you must keep clear of B. If there are no other boats behind B, you could try to slow and tuck in behind B.

• You have no right to room to go between B and the committee boat.

• Next time you want to start at the starboard end, don't get caught in this position!

You are B:
• Before the starting signal, you may luff as high as you like, but you must give A room to keep clear. If you luff slowly at position 1, A has got room, even if he is forced to go the wrong side of the committee boat.

• After the starting signal you must not sail higher than the course which takes you just astern of the committee boat because that's your proper course.

• If you are sailing a straight course which would allow A enough room to sail between you and the committee boat, then to luff at position 2 when he cannot escape would not be giving him room. (Rules 11 and 16 and the definition of 'obstruction'.). So if you want to shut him out, you need to luff at position 1.

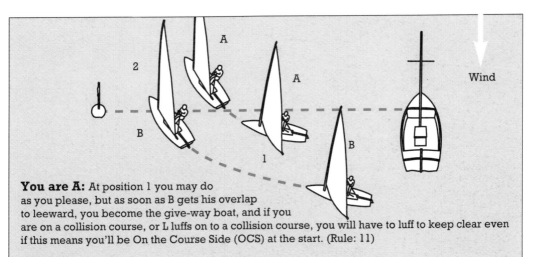

You are A: At position 1 you may do
as you please, but as soon as B gets his overlap
to leeward, you become the give-way boat, and if you
are on a collision course, or L luffs on to a collision course, you will have to luff to keep clear even
if this means you'll be On the Course Side (OCS) at the start. (Rule: 11)

You are B:

• At position 1 you are the give-way boat and must keep clear (Rule 12)

• When you first get the overlap you become the right-of-way boat, but you must give A room to
keep clear. (Rule 15)

• Before the starting signal you may luff up to head-to-wind but you must give A room to keep
clear (Rule 16)

• Immediately after the starting signal you must bear away to a course no higher than close-
hauled. (Rule 17.1)

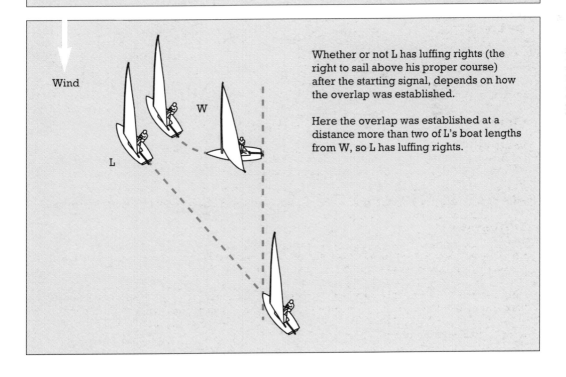

Whether or not L has luffing rights (the
right to sail above his proper course)
after the starting signal, depends on how
the overlap was established.

Here the overlap was established at a
distance more than two of L's boat lengths
from W, so L has luffing rights.

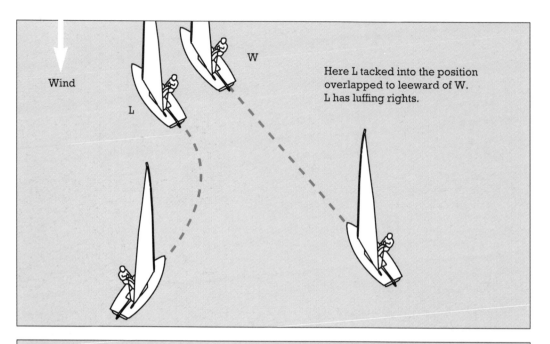

Wind

W

L

Here L tacked into the position overlapped to leeward of W. L has luffing rights.

The diagram opposite shows a reaching start. Before the starting signal (when there is no proper course), all the leeward boats (B,D, F and H) may luff up to head-to-wind, if they can give room to the windward boats to keep clear. At the moment of the starting signal, a boat without luffing rights sailing higher than her proper course must bear away. Assuming that their proper courses are to the right of the picture, which of the leeward boats may luff after the starting signal?

You are A or C or E or G: You must keep clear of the leeward boats under you; and you must keep clear of X coming down the start line on starboard tack, and you must not sail below your proper course. (Rules 11, 10, and 17.2)

Your are B: You established your overlap from clear astern, but you were more than two lengths away from A at the time. You have luffing rights. You may sail higher than your proper course after the start - right up to head-to-wind if A can keep clear. But you must not luff A into the path of X, coming down the start line on starboard tack; in fact you might have to bear away and give more room to A. (Rules 11 and 17.1)

Your are D: You established your overlap from clear astern, and you were within two lengths of C at the time. You are the only leeward boat not to have luffing rights. Before the starting signal (when there is no proper course) you may sail as high as you like, but at the starting signal you must bear away if necessary and then mustn't sail higher than your proper course during the existence of the overlap (unless the gap between the two boats gets to be more than two lengths). (Rules 11 & 17.1)

Your are F: E established the overlap to windward of you, so you have luffing rights. You may sail higher than your proper course after the start - right up to head-to-wind if E can keep clear. (Rule 11)

Your are H: You established your overlap by completing a tack to leeward of G. You have luffing rights. You may sail higher than your proper course after the start - right up to head-to-wind if G can keep clear. (Rule 11)

Your are X: You are not going to be very popular, but as you are on starboard tack you have right-of-way over all the other boats. ('Proper Course' is not relevant when boats are on opposite tacks.) (Rule 10)

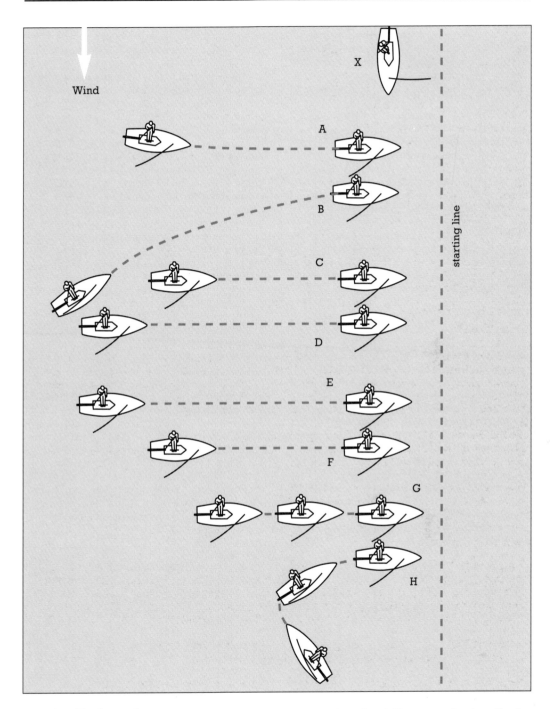

Starting limit marks

Most on-the-water starting lines are between a small buoy (the outer distance mark, or 'ODM'), at the port end, and the mast of a committee boat at the starboard end. These must be described in the sailing instructions. Both the ODM and the committee boat are 'marks' because they have a 'required side' when boats start. The committee boat is also an obstruction, and an inside boat therefore has the right to room when everyone is milling about before the start, but not when boats are approaching the line to start when no-one has the right to room at any starting mark (unless it's not 'surrounded by navigable water').

The most common starting limit mark is the 'inner limit mark' or 'inner distance mark' ('IDM'). Not just the description of the IDM but also the obligations of boats with respect to it must be written into the sailing instructions. You can ignore a sailing instruction like: 'There will be an IDM which will be a yellow mark with a pink flag laid near to the committee boat'.

IDMs cause a lot of problems. The reason they are sometimes used is to try to protect the committee boat, and to prevent sails very close to the committee boat blocking the race committee's view of the starting line.

Let's look at three examples of a limit mark sailing instruction:

1 'A yellow mark with a pink flag will be laid near the committee boat. Boats shall not pass between this mark and the committee boat after the preparatory signal.'
Strictly speaking, such a sailing instruction does not give the mark a required side (rather it specifies a prohibited area which by definition is an obstruction) so it could be argued that you have the right to room to avoid the 'obstruction', and you may hit the buoy without penalty (provided you don't cross the imaginary line between it and any part of the committee boat); and if you are forced into the 'prohibited area' you can escape penalty by protesting the boat

that forced you to infringe the sailing instruction (Rule 60.1(a) gives you the right to a hearing and 64.1(a) exonerates you).

2 The most sensible sailing instruction would be: 'A yellow mark with a pink flag will be laid near the committee boat. Boats shall pass between this mark and the ODM' or 'boats shall pass this mark to starboard'. This would require you to pass the IDM on your starboard side when you are 'approaching the line to start from the pre-course side of the starting line'. Under this sailing instruction, the IDM is a mark because it has a required side, so there is no question of any right to room when you're approaching the line to start. If you get forced the wrong side by someone to leeward who has not infringed a rule (for example by their sailing above close-hauled after the starting signal), then you'll just have to sail back and unwind, and pass it on the correct side.

3 In an attempt to really discourage boats from the area between the IDM and the committee boat, the race committee might write a sailing instruction like this: 'A yellow mark with a pink flag will be placed near the committee boat. Boats shall pass between this mark and the ODM and after the preparatory signal boats shall not pass between this mark and the committee boat'. With this sailing instruction the IDM has a required side, so it is a mark. This means there's no right to room when approaching the line to start and if you get forced between the mark and the line by a boat that didn't infringe a rule, then you'll have to retire. (I don't recommend such a draconian sailing instruction, but I often see them.)

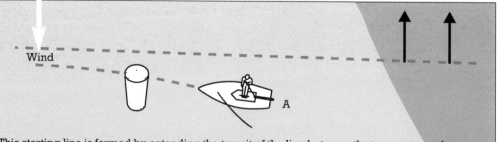

This starting line is formed by extending the transit of the line between the two posts on shore. The ODM has been placed to limit the length of the line.

You are A: When the ODM has drifted behind the line and the port end is favoured, you can gain an advantage. Having passed the ODM on your port side, you'll need to keep sailing towards the line ('approaching the line to start') until you start.

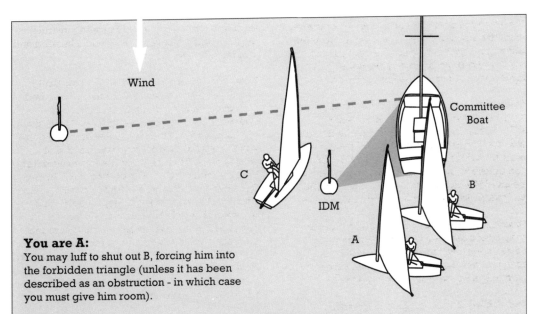

You are A:
You may luff to shut out B, forcing him into
the forbidden triangle (unless it has been
described as an obstruction - in which case
you must give him room).

You are B:
• You must keep clear of A and you cannot claim room if the
IDM has a required side in the sailing instructions. However, if the area between the mark and
the committee boat is simply a prohibited area, then A must give you room (whether you ask for
it or not, but it's best to hail).

• If you hit the mark but pass it on the correct (starboard) side, you can exonerate yourself by
sailing clear and doing a 360 if your only infringement was hitting the mark, or a 720 if you
infringed a 'when boats meet' rule (for example by not keeping clear of A). If you infringed a
'when boats meet' rule and you hit the mark, a 720 will exonerate you for both infringements.

• If you are forced the wrong side of the mark, then whether or not you can successfully protest A,
or exonerate yourself, all depends on the wording of the sailing instruction.

You are C: If this is the best end to start and the IDM is behind the line you can gain something
here by starting right at the end of the line. But having passed the IDM on your starboard side,
you must keep sailing towards the line (or you're no longer 'approaching the line to start') and if
the sailing instruction prohibits you from sailing between the IDM and the committee boat, you'll
need to keep out of the prohibited triangle.

5 The Gate Start

Gate starts are becoming more common in some parts of the world as a way of starting more than eighty or so boats, in a fairly steady wind of Force 3 or more, when there is sufficient room on the water. Discussion will never cease as to whether the gate start or the line start is the fairer, but there is no doubt that gate starts can be exciting, and require a different expertise to do well.

This is how a gate start works. A path-finder is appointed. Usually it is one of the competing boats near the top of the fleet. Just before the

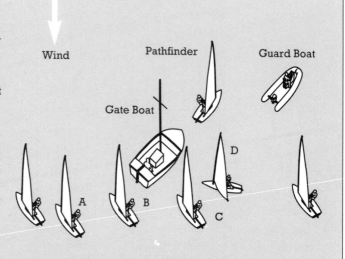

starting signal he sets off on a port tack close-hauled course. A guard boat is sometimes used, to motor along on the pathfinder's starboard bow, to ensure other boats don't run into the pathfinder and ruin the whole proceedings.

A gate boat takes up a position astern of the pathfinder, exactly matching the pathfinder's speed and course. Boats then start on starboard tack behind the gate boat. Those that think they sail faster than the pathfinder or think the left side of the beat is best start early (near the beginning of the run), those that think the pathfinder sails faster than they do, or think the right side of the beat is best wait around where they expect the entourage to be five minutes or so after the starting signal. Knowing the exact time is unimportant; the skill is in 'coming out of the gate' close-hauled at full speed, by luffing from a reach to close-hauled missing the starboard quarter of the gate-boat by a few millimetres. The pathfinder is released usually after five minutes; he can tack any time after being released, gaining a few boat lengths by not having to sail behind the gate boat - a reward for being forced to start at the extreme right side of the beat, and not being allowed to tack on any shifts for the first five minutes.

You are A or B:
• This is really just the same situation as the starboard end of a fixed starting line. You have to keep clear of a boat to leeward, and you have right-of-way over a boat to windward. You must also keep clear of the gate boat.

You are C:
• If you can sail close-hauled without changing course, then you can ignore D. Or you can luff D to force him to luff alongside the gate boat, but you can't luff him into the gate boat, because if you luff you must give him room to keep clear. (Rule 16)

You are D:
• You will need to slow, not to go behind C as you would if this were a fixed-line start, but to be level with him, as are A and B. Remember, the gate-boat is moving at the speed of the pathfinder. You must keep clear of the gate boat. If you touch the gate boat (or the guard boat or - heaven forbid - the pathfinder), you must retire (no chance of a 720) unless you think it wasn't your fault. For example if C forces you to collide with the gate boat by luffing you can hail "protest", display a protest flag, sail on, and lodge a protest after the race.

6 On the Beat

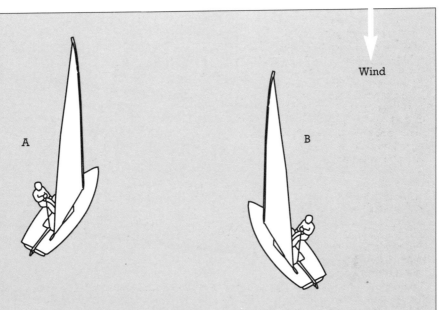

Wind

A

B

You are A:
• Your obligation is simple: to keep clear. (Rule 10)

• If you are going to bear away behind B, you must do it in such away that B is left in no doubt that you are going to succeed. (Rule 10)

If you decide to tack, you must complete the tack ahead or to leeward of B without B having to alter course until your tack is complete. If there is any doubt about whether you tacked far enough from B, a protest hearing is likely to go against you. (Rule 13)

You are B:
• You are not required to hail 'starboard' or anything else, but it is sometimes a good idea to do so if you think that A hasn't seen you because:

1. You must try to avoid contact, and if there is contact and there is damage, you may be penalised. (Rule 14)

2. Even if there is no chance of damage, getting tangled up with a boat required to keep clear can cost many boatlengths and no redress can be claimed for places lost, (unless you are actually damaged by the give-way boat). (Rules 14, 16, 62.1(b))

• If you want to continue on starboard tack, and don't want A tacking into a position which forces you (from a tactical point of view) to tack, you may bear away and go behind A. You could shout 'Carry on', or 'Pass ahead of me' but nothing you shout puts any obligation on A which he doesn't already have. Although a firm bear-away and/or a hail will often make A decide to carry on, if A is an experienced and skilled racing sailor and is determined to force you into a tactically disadvantageous position, it is not easy to prevent him.

When A completes his tack he is overlapped to leeward of B.

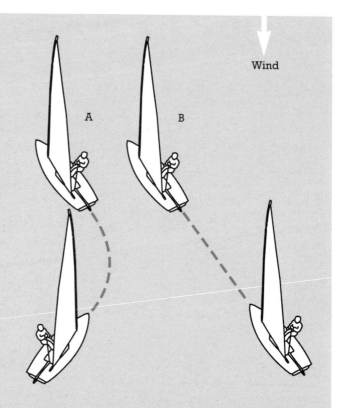

Wind

You are A:

• As you approach on port tack your obligation is simple - to keep clear of B. (Rule 10)

• While you are tacking (until you are close-hauled on the new tack) you must keep clear of B. (Rule 13)

• When your tack is complete, you become the right-of-way boat, but it is only at that instant that B has to begin to take any avoiding action, so you mustn't be in a position where it is impossible or difficult for B to keep clear. Remember, he doesn't have to anticipate that you are going to be there. If he is able to keep clear only with difficulty, then your tack was too close. (Rule 15)

• When your tack is complete, you have luffing rights, but you cannot use them until you have given B room to keep clear (which requires both space and time). After giving B this opportunity, you may luff above close-hauled if you want to, but your luff must be such that B is able to keep clear. (Rule 16)

You are B:

• You must give A room to keep clear. In other words you must not alter course if by so doing you prevent A from keeping clear, or make it difficult for him to keep clear. If there is a header (adverse windshift) just as A is tacking, you may be prevented from fulfilling your wish to bear away for a few seconds. You must not alter course if by doing so you make it impossible or difficult for A to keep clear. You may, of course, tack while A is tacking. (Rule 16)

• You may alter course towards A as he approaches on port tack (whether or not there is a windshift), forcing A has to tack earlier, provided A can keep clear without difficulty. (Rule 16)

• Once A's tack is complete and he is to leeward, you become the give-way yacht, and you must keep clear. As you will be affected by his back-wind, it's usually tactically sound to tack. (Rule 11)

• Remember that A has luffing rights; once he has given you the opportunity to keep clear he may luff.

• You are not prohibited from tacking, even if A has altered course to keep clear, provided that A has room to keep clear.

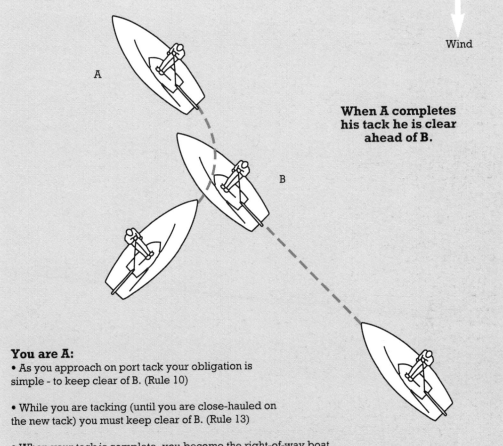

Wind

When A completes his tack he is clear ahead of B.

You are A:
• As you approach on port tack your obligation is simple - to keep clear of B. (Rule 10)

• While you are tacking (until you are close-hauled on the new tack) you must keep clear of B. (Rule 13)

• When your tack is complete, you become the right-of-way boat, but it is only at that instant that B has to begin to take any avoiding action, so you mustn't be in a position where it is impossible or difficult for B to keep clear. Remember, he doesn't have to anticipate that you are going to be there. If he is able to keep clear only with difficulty, then your tack was too close. (Rule 15)

• When you complete your tack you may be sailing more slowly than B, and if B establishes an overlap to leeward of you, you become the give-way boat again, and you must keep clear. However, B must not sail above close-hauled unless he tacks away under your stern. (Rules 11 & 17.1)

You are B:
• You must give A room to keep clear. In other words you must not alter course if by so doing you prevent A from keeping clear, or make it difficult for him to keep clear. If there is a lift (beneficial windshift) just as A is passing ahead, you may be prevented from fulfilling your wish to luff for a few seconds. (Rule 16)

• You are not prohibited from altering course provided that you don't prevent A from keeping clear or make it difficult for him to keep clear. (Rule 16)

• Provided you don't obstruct A, you can tack away at any time. If you get an overlap to leeward of A, after his tack is complete, you may not sail above close hauled unless you tack away under his stern. (Rule 17.1)

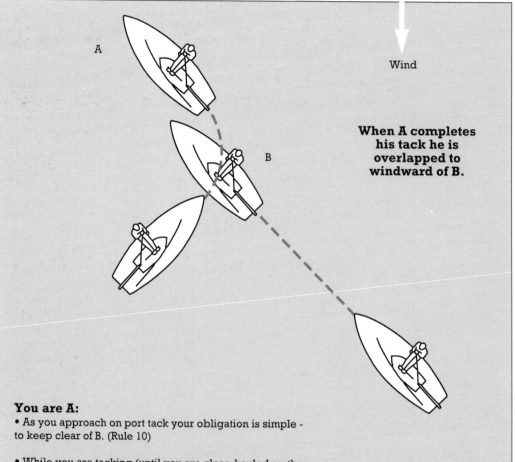

When A completes his tack he is overlapped to windward of B.

You are A:

• As you approach on port tack your obligation is simple - to keep clear of B. (Rule 10)

• While you are tacking (until you are close-hauled on the new tack) you must keep clear of B. (Rule 13)

• When your tack is complete, are overlapped on B's windward bow putting B in your wind shadow. This is known as a 'slam dunk'. You are still the give-way boat. Furthermore, B has luffing rights and may luff above close-hauled. You must keep clear. (Rule 11)

You are B:

• You must give A room to keep clear. In other words you must not alter course if by so doing you prevent A from keeping clear, or make it difficult for him to keep clear. If there is a lift (beneficial windshift) just as A is passing ahead, you may be prevented from fulfilling your wish to luff for a few seconds. (Rule 16)

• You are not prohibited from altering course provided that you don't prevent A from keeping clear or make it difficult for him to keep clear. (Rule 16)

• If at the completion of A's tack you are overlapped to leeward of A, then you have luffing rights, and may luff above close-hauled, but you must give A a chance to keep clear. (Rule 16)

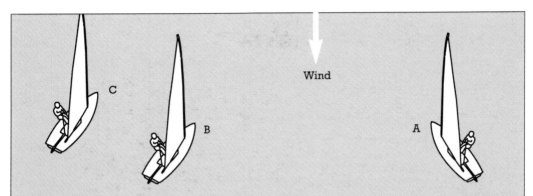

You are A:
• Your rights and obligations are exactly the same as those of boat B on page 29.

You are B:
• You must keep clear of A. (Rule 10)

• You have the right to choose either to go under A's stern, or, as you need to make a substantial alteration of course to avoid A, to tack, irrespective of any hail from C. (Rule 19.1)

• If you decide to go behind A you must allow C room to pass under A's stern should he also choose to do so (though unless you are in a team race and C is an opponent, he'd probably rather tack). (Rule 18.2(a))

• If you decide to tack, you must hail C (something like 'room to tack' or 'water for a starboard boat') and then begin your tacking manoeuvre as soon as you can do so without colliding with C. You need to hail early enough to allow C time to respond to your hail before you have a problem with A. This is especially important if there are boats to windward of C. (Rule 19.1)

• You must not hail for C to tack, and then go behind A (unless C does not respond to the hail). (Rule 19.1)

• If you decide to hail for room to tack, and C does not respond, hail again louder. The key issue in protests, in situations like this, is often whether or not the hail was made; the helmsman of the leeward boat says he hailed, and the helmsman of the hailed boat says he never heard a hail. The protest committee will be more inclined to find as fact that a hail was made, if it is repeated, louder.

• If you can keep clear of A by making only a small (or no) alteration of course, then you do not have the right to hail and must pass under A, giving room to C if he chooses to go under A as well. (Rules 18.2(a), 19.1, Definition of Obstruction, ISAF Case 6)

You are C:
• Obviously you may tack if you want to.

• You must keep clear of A, and as windward boat you must keep clear of B if he luffs. If B sails behind A, then provided that in your opinion (you must be reasonable) you cannot safely cross in front of A, you have the right to go behind A, and B must give you room (whether you ask for it or not) provided you had an inside overlap when B was two lengths from A. (Rules 10 & 11)

• If B hails for room to tack, then you must either immediately tack, or hail 'you tack' and take on the responsibility of keeping clear. If you choose to tack, you don't have to carry out the tack any faster than is normal for you, but you must begin the manoeuvre immediately. You are under no obligation to tack unless B hails for room. (Rule 19.1)

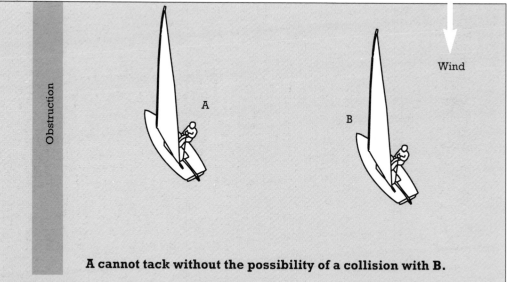

A cannot tack without the possibility of a collision with B.

You are A:

• You will need room to tack, and you know that if you do B will be in the way, so you have the right to hail B for room to tack. (Rule 19.1)

• You are permitted to hail only if you really believe there is an obstruction ahead, but underwater weed or shallows count as an obstruction.

• Until you hail, B is under no obligation to do anything. (Rule 19.1)

• If he doesn't respond to the first hail, hail again more loudly.

• If there is a boat to windward or astern of B that would prevent him from tacking, you will need to hail in time for him to hail for room. (Rule 19.1)

• If he responds by tacking, you must tack as soon as there is room for you to complete your tack even if there is a lift (advantageous wind-shift) and you'd like to change your mind and continue sailing near the shore out of an adverse tide. (Rule 19.1(a))

• If he responds by hailing something like 'you tack', you must immediately tack. (Rule 19.1(b))

You are B:

• You must keep clear if A luffs to head-to-wind because you will be windward or astern. (Rules 11 & 12)

• Although you are under no obligation to do anything until A hails, if it's windy and noisy, you should be reasonably attentive to his desire to hail.

• In response to his hail you must immediately either tack as soon as possible, or hail back 'you tack'.

• If you want to tack but cannot tack because of a boat to windward or astern, you must hail that boat for room to tack and tack as soon as you can. (Rule 19)

• If you hail 'you tack' you undertake to keep clear of A while he tacks, and having completed his tack, you have to give him a chance to keep clear without difficulty. (Rule 19.1(b))

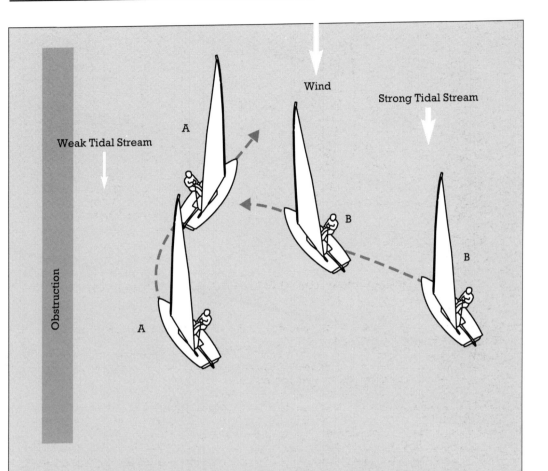

A wants to tack but is unsure whether he can tack and clear B.
So A has the right to hail B for room to tack. He hails "Room to tack".
B replies "Carry on".

You are A:
• If there is room, you must tack immediately, even if there is a lift (advantageous wind-shift)
and you'd like to continue sailing near the shore out of the adverse tidal stream. (Rule 19.1(a))

• When you have completed your tack you become the give-way boat and you must try to keep
clear of B. In this diagram there is nothing you can do except sail straight on, so you can sail on
and you have broken no rule. (Rule 10)

You are B:
When you hail "You tack" you undertake to keep clear of A while he tacks, and having
completed his tack, you have to give him a chance to keep clear without difficulty. You can
give A room by bearing off behind him. If you do so, no rule is broken. (Rule 19.1(b))

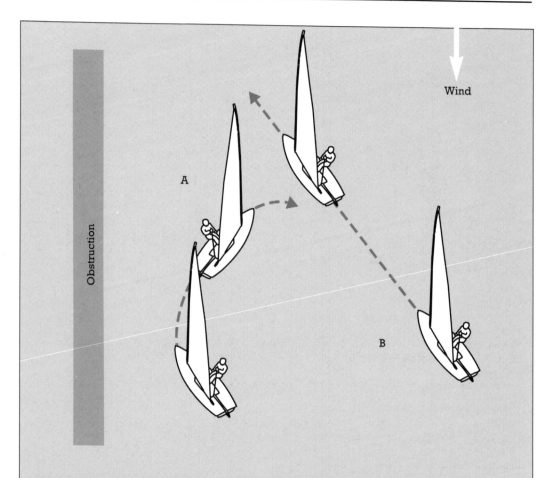

A wants to tack but is unsure whether he can tack and clear B. So A has the right to hail B for room to tack. A hails "Room to tack". B replies "Carry on".

You are A:

• You must tack immediately, even if there is a lift (advantageous windshift) and you'd like to continue sailing near the shore. (Rule 19.1(a))

• When you have completed your tack you become the give-way boat and you must try to keep clear of B. If you can bear away under B's stern without difficulty (as you can in this diagram), then you must do so. You become required to keep clear only when your tack is complete, and if you then cannot keep clear, or you manage to keep clear but only by making an unseaman-like manoeuvre, then B has broken a rule and you should protest. (Rules 10 & 19.1(b))

You are B:

When you hail "You tack" you undertake to keep clear of A while he tacks, but having completed his tack, you have to give him a chance to keep clear without difficulty. In this diagram you have done so; A can easily bear off behind you, so no rule is broken. (Rules 10 & 19.1(b))

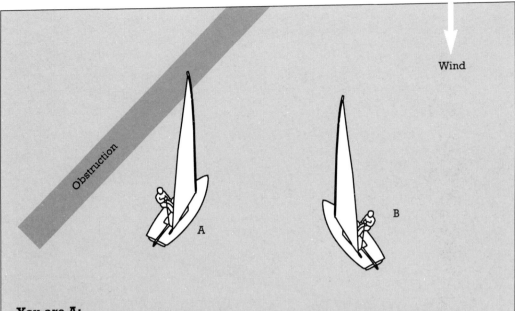

You are A:
• You are in big trouble. You don't have the right to room, and the obstruction prevents you from tacking. If you force B to alter course, you must take a 720 penalty. (Rules 10 & 44.1)

• You should have thought of this possibilty earlier when there was time to bear away under B!

You are B:
• You could be Mr. Nice Guy and tack now, or you could sail on till you are forced to tack to avoid contact with A, in which case A will have broken a rule. (Rule 10)

7 Rounding the Windward Mark

Rounding a port-hand windward mark

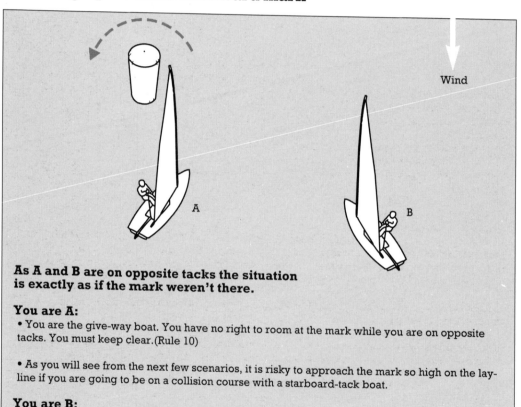

As A and B are on opposite tacks the situation is exactly as if the mark weren't there.

You are A:
• You are the give-way boat. You have no right to room at the mark while you are on opposite tacks. You must keep clear.(Rule 10)

• As you will see from the next few scenarios, it is risky to approach the mark so high on the lay-line if you are going to be on a collision course with a starboard-tack boat.

You are B:
• You are the right-of-way boat, but any alteration of course must be such that A is able to keep clear. (Rule 16)

A tacks into a position overlapped to leeward of B, completing his tack when more than two lengths from the mark.

You are A:
• As you approach on port tack, you are the give-way boat and must keep clear. (Rule 10)

• While you are tacking you are the give-way boat and must keep clear. (Rule 13)

• You have completed the tack just outside two boat-lengths, and you are overlapped inside B. You

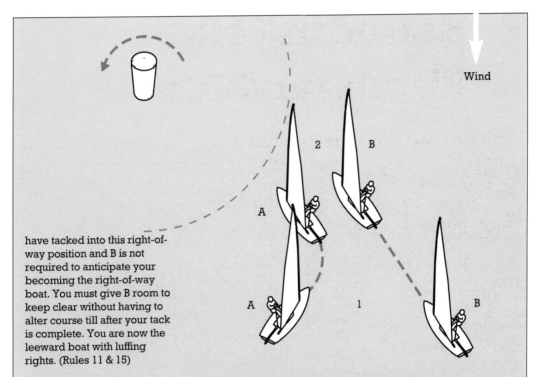

have tacked into this right-of-way position and B is not required to anticipate your becoming the right-of-way boat. You must give B room to keep clear without having to alter course till after your tack is complete. You are now the leeward boat with luffing rights. (Rules 11 & 15)

• Having given B room to keep clear, without having had to anticipate, you may luff at any time (you may need to luff above close-hauled to squeeze round the mark) or continue on a close-hauled course straight past the mark, or bear off round the mark, but if you luff you must give B room to keep clear. (Rule 11)

• Only if your only proper course is to gybe around the mark must you not sail higher than your proper course as you round the mark. (Rule 18.4)

• If B is not able to keep clear because there are several other boats to windward of him, then you do not have the right to tack under him and sail your proper course round the mark. (Rule 18.2)

• If there is 'reasonable doubt' as to whether either of you were two lengths from the mark when your tack was complete, you must presume that you are too late to get the right to round inside B. (Rule 18.2(c))

You are B:
• While A is approaching on port tack and while he's tacking you mustn't alter course to prevent him from keeping clear or make it difficult for him to keep clear. This doesn't stop you bearing away early to force him to tack earlier to avoid you, provided he can do it without difficulty. (Rules 13 & 16)

• If you are forced to alter course before A has completed his tack, A will have broken rule 13.

• However, if A completes his tack outside two boat-lengths, then he becomes the right of way boat, and you must keep clear. He has luffing rights and unless his only proper course is to gybe around the mark, he may luff at any time or sail straight on. You must keep clear. (Rules 11 & 18.2(a))

• If you believe A's tack was completed when either of you were within two lengths of the mark, then A has no right to round inside you. You can protest but you should still keep clear. (Rules 18.2(c) & 11)

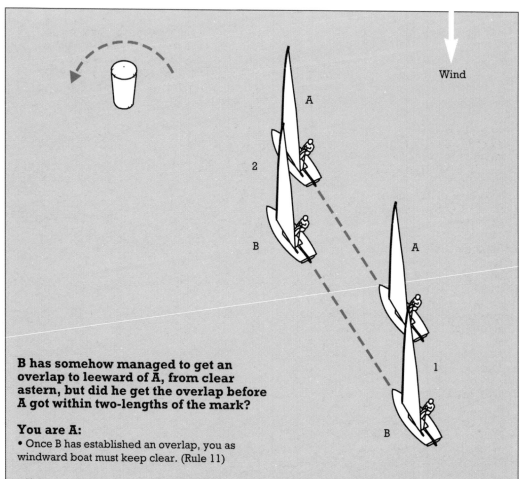

B has somehow managed to get an overlap to leeward of A, from clear astern, but did he get the overlap before A got within two-lengths of the mark?

You are A:
• Once B has established an overlap, you as windward boat must keep clear. (Rule 11)

• If there is doubt as to whether the overlap was established before you were within two lengths then B does not have the right to round inside. It is a good idea to tell him so. (Rule 18.2(c))

• Because B got his overlap from clear astern, he has no luffing rights, but when the overlap is established before you were two lengths from the mark, then he may sail his proper course around the mark, and you must keep clear. His proper course is a wide rounding if that's how he would round without you being there. You must keep clear. (Rule 18.2(a))

You are B:
• If you establish the overlap, without doubt, before A comes within two lengths of the mark, you have the right to sail your proper course as you round the mark. This means you may sail the course you would have sailed in the absence of A. If these means sailing above close-hauled (to 'shoot' the mark) then that's OK. If you want to head up a bit so that you don't get too far from the mark as you complete the rounding, that's OK too. (Rule 18.2(a))

• If there is 'reasonable doubt' as to whether A was two lengths from the mark when you established the overlap, you must presume that you are too late. If A is shouting to you that your overlap is too late, you'd be wise to keep clear. (Rule 18.2(c))

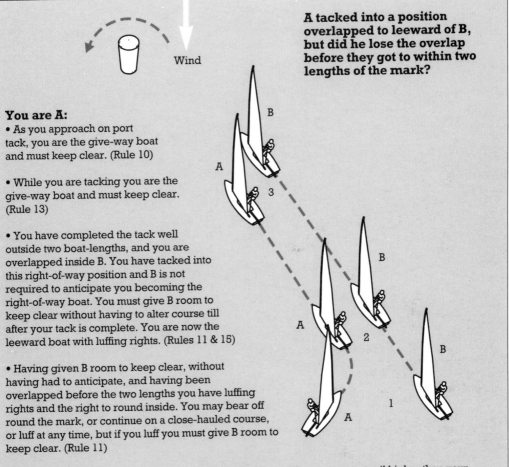

A tacked into a position
overlapped to leeward of B,
but did he lose the overlap
before they got to within two
lengths of the mark?

You are A:

• As you approach on port
tack, you are the give-way boat
and must keep clear. (Rule 10)

• While you are tacking you are the
give-way boat and must keep clear.
(Rule 13)

• You have completed the tack well
outside two boat-lengths, and you are
overlapped inside B. You have tacked into
this right-of-way position and B is not
required to anticipate you becoming the
right-of-way boat. You must give B room to
keep clear without having to alter course till
after your tack is complete. You are now the
leeward boat with luffing rights. (Rules 11 & 15)

• Having given B room to keep clear, without
having had to anticipate, and having been
overlapped before the two lengths you have luffing
rights and the right to round inside. You may bear off
round the mark, or continue on a close-hauled course,
or luff at any time, but if you luff you must give B room to
keep clear. (Rule 11)

• Only if your only proper course is to gybe around the mark must you not sail higher than your
proper course as you round the mark. (Rule 18.4)

• If there is 'reasonable doubt' as to whether either of you were two lengths from the mark when your
tack was complete, you can presume that you have not lost the right to round inside. (Rule 18.2(c))

You are B:

• While A is approaching on port tack and while he's tacking you mustn't alter course to prevent him
from keeping clear or make it difficult for him to keep clear. This doesn't stop you bearing away
early to force him to tack earlier to avoid you, provided he can do it without difficulty. (Rules 13 & 16)

• If you are forced to alter course before A has completed his tack, A will have broken rule 13.

• As A completes his tack outside two boat-lengths, he becomes the right of way boat, and you must
keep clear. He has luffing rights and unless his only proper course is to gybe around the mark, he
may luff at any time or sail straight on. You must keep clear. (Rules 11 & 18.2(a))

• If there is doubt as to whether you have broken the overlap when you come within two lengths of
the mark, then A has the right to round inside you. If A is shouting to you that he is overlapped at two
lengths, you'd be wise to keep clear. (Rule 18.2(c))

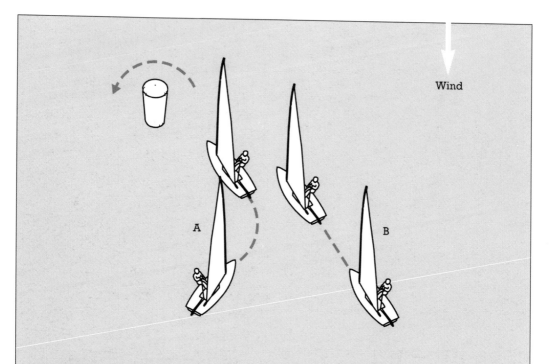

Wind

A

B

A completes his tack on to starboard within two lengths of the mark, ahead or to leeward of B.

You are A:

• As you approach on port tack, you are the give-way boat and must keep clear. (Rule 10)

• While you are tacking you are the give-way boat and must keep clear. (Rule 13)

• You have completed the tack within two boatlengths of the mark. You have tacked into this right-of-way position but B is not required to anticipate your having become the right-of-way boat. You must give B room to keep clear without having to alter course till after your tack is complete. (Rule 15)

• Now you have another problem. You must also not force B (who is probably sailing faster than you are) to luff above close-hauled in order to avoid you (even after your tack is complete). (Rule 18.3(a))

You are B:

• While A is approaching on port tack and while he's tacking you mustn't alter course to prevent him from keeping clear or make it difficult for him to keep clear. This doesn't stop you bearing away early to force him to tack earlier to avoid you, provided he can do it without difficulty. (Rules 13 & 16)

• If you are forced to alter course before A has completed his tack, A will have broken rule 13.

• If A completes his tack to leeward of you he becomes the right of way boat, but if you can avoid him only by sailing above close-hauled (which is almost inevitable in this diagram) then he has broken rule 18.3(a) and must take a penalty.

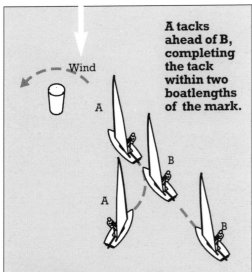

A tacks ahead of B, completing the tack within two boatlengths of the mark.

You are A:

• As you tack you must keep clear of B. (Rules 13 & 15)

• If you complete your tack without forcing B to alter course to avoid you, the next thing you have to worry about is that if B, with superior speed, can avoid you only by sailing above his close-hauled course, then you have broken a rule, and must take a penalty. (Rule 18.3(a))

• Furthermore, if B chooses to bear away and get an overlap to leeward of you, you must keep clear while B rounds the mark. (Rule 18.3(b))

• Even if B does not get an overlap, you must stay clear until B has completed his rounding. (Rule 18.3(a))

• Basically, for this manoeuvre to succeed, you must stay clear ahead until B has competed his rounding (that is, until B has left the mark astern).

You are B:

• When A's tack is complete, you become the give-way boat, but if the only way you can avoid him is to luff, he has broken a rule and must take a penalty. (Rule 18.3(a))

• If you choose to bear away and get an overlap to leeward of A, A must keep clear while you round the mark. You mustn't sail higher than your proper course. (Rules 17.1 & 18.3(b))

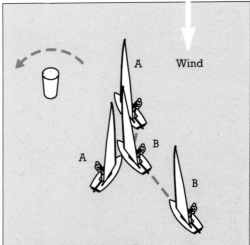

A completes his tack within two lengths of the mark nearly overlapped, or overlapped to windward of B.

You are A:

• As you tack you must keep clear of B. (Rule 13)

• If at the moment you pass through head-to-wind B is overlapped to leeward, then B has luffing rights. You must continue to keep clear of B even if B luffs right up to head-to-wind. (Rule 11)

• If at the moment your tack is complete B is clear astern, and chooses to go between you and the mark, you must keep clear of B who is allowed to sail his proper course (the course he would have sailed had you not been there). (Rule 18.3(b))

You are B:

• If you were clear astern when A completed his tack, you may choose to go inside if you want to, and then sail your proper course (the course you would have sailed had A not been there). (Rule 18.3(b))

• If you were overlapped to leeward of A when A completed his tack, you have luffing rights and you may sail any course, but if you luff you must allow A room to keep clear. However, if your only proper course is to gybe at the mark, you can sail your proper course but no higher. (Rules 11 & 18.4)

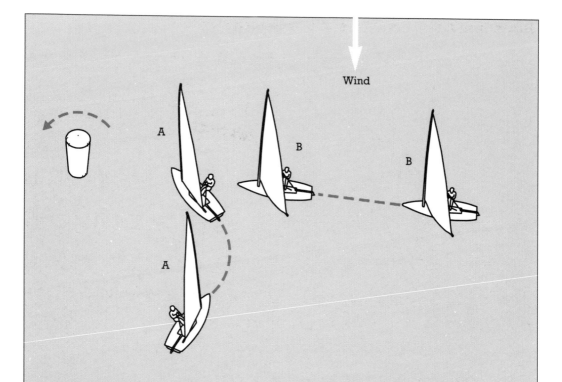

Wind

A tacks within two lengths of the mark to leeward or ahead of B who is approaching on a reach (perhaps having overstood the mark).

You are A:
• You must complete your tack without B having to alter course to keep clear. (Rule 13)

• After you have completed your tack, you mustn't force B to sail above his close-hauled course in order to keep clear of you. (Rule 18.3(a))

• Even though you have luffing rights, you must just sail your proper course and not prevent B from passing the mark. (Rule 18.3(a))

• Once B has passed the mark (left it astern) you may luff (you have luffing rights). (Rule 11)

You are B:
• You need do nothing till A's tack is complete, then you must keep clear, but if the only way you can keep clear is by sailing above close-hauled, then A must take a 720 degree penalty. (Rule 18.3(a))

• A has luffing rights but must not sail above his proper course until you have passed the mark (that is, left it astern). (Rules 11 & 18.3(a))

Rounding a starboard-hand windward mark

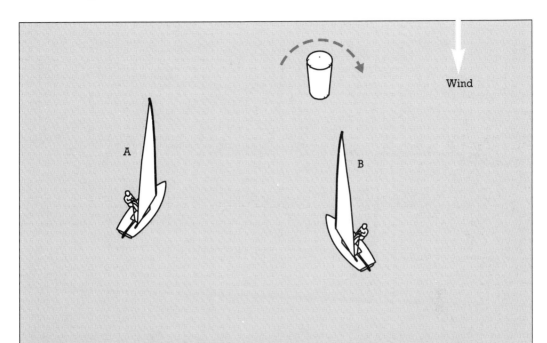

A and B are on opposite tacks so the situation is exactly as if the mark wasn't there.

You are A:
You are the give-way boat. You have no right to room at the mark. You must keep clear. (Rule 10)

You are B:
You hold right-of-way, but any alteration of course must be such that A is able to keep clear. (Rule 16)

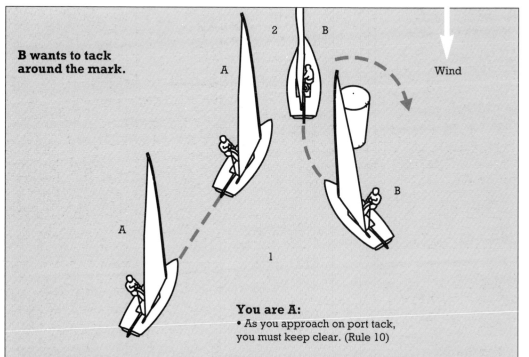

B wants to tack around the mark.

Wind

You are A:
• As you approach on port tack, you must keep clear. (Rule 10)

• At position 2, B has luffed to head-to-wind. He is still on starboard tack. You must keep clear. (Rule 10)

• If you keep clear by luffing, you must not end up so close along side him, that any alteration of course he makes will result in immediately making contact. (Rule 11 and the Definition of 'Keep Clear'.)

• If you luff and tack, you must keep clear. (Rule 13)

You are B:
• As A approaches you must not alter course so as to make it difficult for A to keep clear. However, the luff to get to position 2 in has fulfilled this obligation, as A can easily keep clear by luffing. (Rule 16)

• At position 2 you must not turn any more, because once you go through head-to-wind you become the give-way boat, and A is so close behind that he will be forced to alter course. (Rule 13)

• If A ducks your stern, leaving the mark on the wrong side, you'll probably be able to tack but you will be the give-way boat while you're tacking, and you'll probably be the windward boat when you've completed your tack. In either case you must keep clear. (Rules 13 & 11)

• If A luffs to avoid you when you're head-to-wind, and gets overlapped on your port side, although you remain the right-of-way boat till he goes through head-to-wind, you cannot alter course to make it difficult for him to keep clear. (Rule 16)

• If A tacks, then immediately he is past head-to-wind you can complete your tack.(Rule 13)

• The best tactic in this scenario if you haven't room to complete a tack before A gets too close, is to slow down at position 1 to force A to tack, then tack.

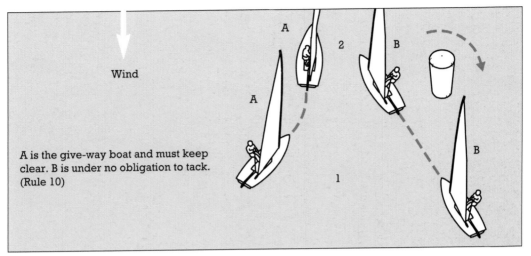

A is the give-way boat and must keep
clear. B is under no obligation to tack.
(Rule 10)

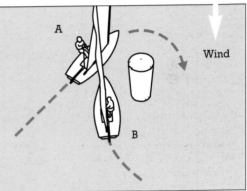

You are A:
You were keeping clear of B by passing
ahead. He is not allowed to obstruct you.
(Rule 16)

You are B:
As much as you may like to luff to tack
around the mark, you cannot do this if the
change of course prevents A from keeping
clear, or makes it difficult for him to keep
clear. (Rule 16)

You are A:
• At position 1 when you begin to luff to tack, you are clear
ahead and, therefore, the right-of-way boat.

• When you go through head-to-wind you must keep clear of B.
Because B has luffed you may be prevented from completing
your tack. (Rule 13)

• Next time you approach the mark with an opponent close astern,
try to be on the layline, rather than half a length to leeward.

You are B:
• As A luffs to head-to-wind, you may luff too. You don't have to
anticipate that he is going to tack.

• When A goes through head-to-wind you become the right-of-
way boat, so if you change course after he goes through head-
to-wind, you must not prevent him from keeping clear or make it difficult to keep clear. (Rule 16)

• To prevent A from tacking in front of you, you need to luff till he reaches head-to-wind,
then sail straight.

When the windward mark is an obstruction

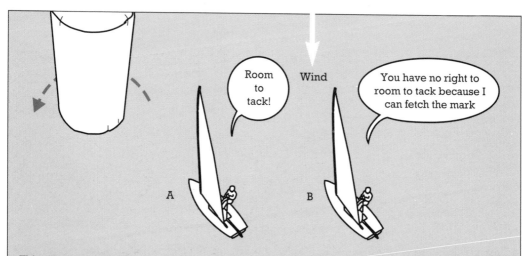

This situation occurs only when the mark is also an obstruction (but not if it's a starting mark when approaching the line to start). This is fairly unusual, and the obligations and rights are not easy to remember, so if you're new to racing don't bother with this part just yet!

You are A:
• Provided that you are on a collision course for the obstruction, you may hail to B for room to tack. "Water" may be misunderstood, "Room to tack" is best. (Rule 19.1)

• If B chooses not to tack (he should inform you by shouting something like "refused") and then fails to fetch the mark (that is, he goes beyond head-to-wind to get round), then he has infringed and you should protest him. (Rule 19.2)

• Even if B can get round the mark without going beyond head-to-wind, you are still the right-of-way boat provided you don't go beyond head-to-wind yourself, so even if you don't have luffing rights, you may go up to head-to-wind in order to 'shoot the mark', and he must keep clear. (Rule 11)

• For you to have the right to hail, you have to be on a course from which you must make a substantial alteration to avoid the obstruction. If you were further to leeward, so that the obstruction was not in your path, then you would not have the right to hail; you would have to slow down and tack behind B or bear off and gybe. (Definition of 'obstruction')

You are B:
• As the windward boat you must keep clear, if A luffs in an attempt to 'shoot the mark'. (Rule 11)

• If A hails for room to tack, and you are sure that you can get round the mark without tacking, then you may refuse to tack, but if he luffs remember you are the windward boat and must keep clear. (Rule 11)

• If A hails for room to tack, and you are not sure that you can get round the mark without tacking, then you must either tack or hail back 'you tack' and give room to A to tack. (Rule 19)

8 On the Reach

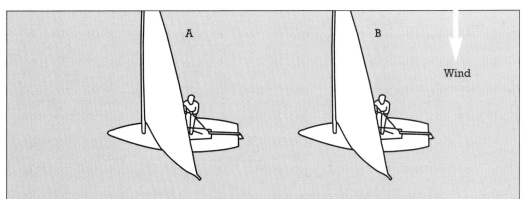

Wind

You are A: You are the right-of-way boat and you may alter course as you please.

You are B: Your only obligation is to keep clear of A (because you are 'clear astern'), but you may sail any course you like. (Rule 11)

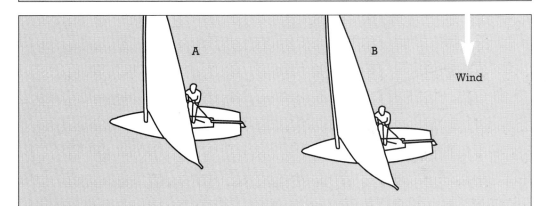

Wind

You are A:
• If B is within two boatlengths of you and heading towards your leeward side, you must not sail below your proper course (see the definition of proper course on pages 12 & 13). (Rule 17.2)

• If there are waves to be played, you can play them. If there are boats to windward or astern likely to take your wind, you can bear away to get clear air. You simply mustn't sail lower than you would have done in the absence of B. (Rules 12 & 17.2)

You are B:
• As you are the boat clear astern, you must keep clear of A, but while there is no overlap you have no other obligations and may alter course as you please. (Rule 12)

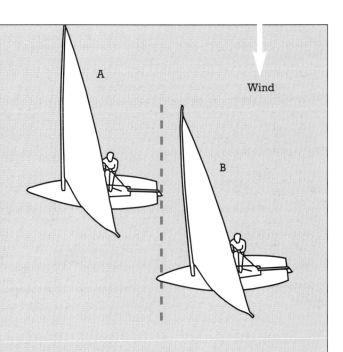

You are A:

• After B gets an overlap, you continue to be required not to sail below your proper course, but you now have a new obligation - to keep clear, even if B sails a course higher than your own. (Rules 17.2 & 11)

• If B sails a course you think is higher than his proper course, you may protest, but you must still keep clear. (Rule 11)

• If B sails very low (in an effort to hold on to clear wind), you continue to be obliged not to sail below your proper course while the gap between you is anything up to two boatlengths. (Rules 11 & 17.2)

You are B:

• When you get your overlap to leeward of A, you will become right-of-way boat, but A doesn't have to anticipate your getting the overlap, so you must initially give him room to keep clear. (Rule 15)

• Once you've done this, although you don't have luffing rights, you may sail up to, but not above, your proper course. You must not sail above your proper course while the overlap exists and you are within two boatlengths of A. (Rules 11 & 17.1)

• If you luff (up to your proper course), you must give A room to keep clear. (Rule 16)

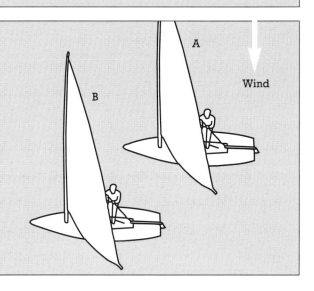

B having established an overlap to leeward of A, has somehow advanced nearly a boatlength through A's lee. There is no change in rights and obligations. B may sail as high as his proper course, and A must keep clear. A might be forced to sail higher than **his** proper course, but he must keep clear because it's B's proper course that counts.

The boats are in the same positions as they were in the previous diagram, but here the situation has arisen through A establishing an over-lap from astern to windward of B. The boats' rights and obligations are quite different, because B has luffing rights.

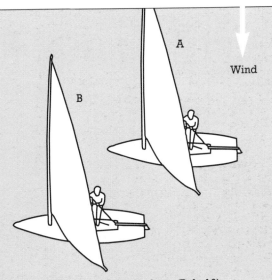

You are A:
• You must keep clear of B. (Rule 11)

• You must not sail below your proper course whilst the overlap exits (and the gap between the two boats is less than two lengths). (Rule 17.2)

You are B:
• You may sail any course, but if you luff you must give A room to keep clear. (Rule 16)

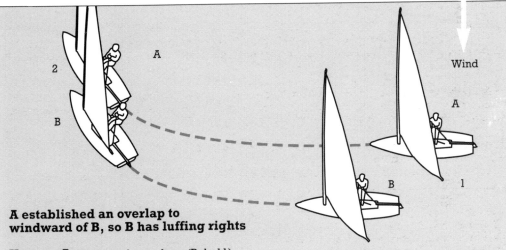

A established an overlap to windward of B, so B has luffing rights

You are A: You must keep clear. (Rule 11)

You are B: You may luff or bear away as you please provided you give A room to keep clear. (Rule 16)

The 'lock-up' position:
• At position 2, if A luffs, his stern will swing into B. If he bears away their courses will converge and there will be contact almost immediately. The only way in which A can fulfil his obligation to keep clear is to sail straight on. B can luff no more, for to do so would not be giving A room to keep clear. B may continue sailing straight ahead, or he may bear away. (Rules 11 & 16)

• It is for this reason that luffing a boat to windward is rarely worthwhile in fleet racing. B would be wise to luff to clear his wind before A gets an overlap to windward and, unless there is a port rounding mark coming up soon, encourage A to overtake to leeward.

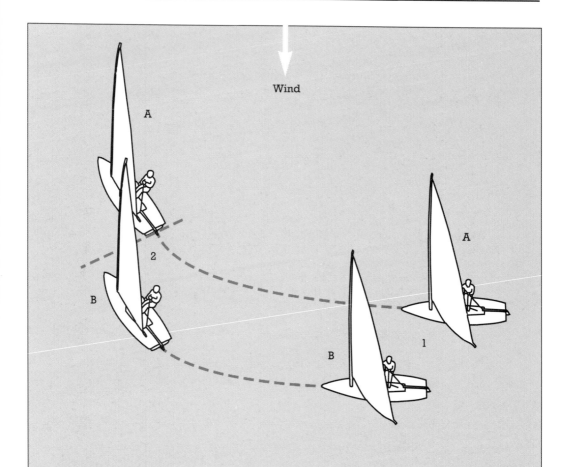

A establishes an overlap to windward of B. At position 2 the overlap is broken.

You are A:

• Position 1: You established the overlap from clear astern to windward of B, so B has luffing rights. You must keep clear. (Rule 11)

• Position 2: When the overlap is broken, your only obligation is not to sail below your proper course, unless you gybe. (Rule 17.2)

You are B:

• Position 1: You have luffing rights and may luff as high as you please but you must give A room to keep clear. (Rule 16)

• Position 2: When A draws ahead and the overlap is broken, you become clear-astern and must therefore keep clear, but you may sail any course. (Rule 12)

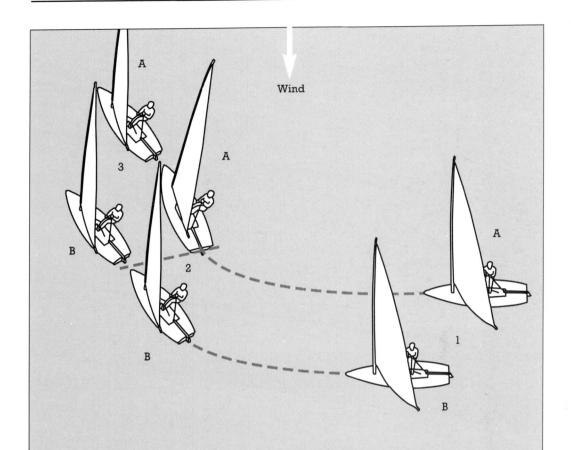

A established the overlap to windward of B.

You are A:
• Position 1: You established the overlap from clear astern to windward of B, so B has luffing rights. You must keep clear. (Rule 11)

• Position 2: You can luff to break the overlap so that B loses his luffing rights.

• Position 3: When you bear away and an overlap is re-established, B must bear away to his proper course (or lower). However, you are still the give-way boat and must keep clear. (Rule 11)

You are B:
• Position 1: You have luffing rights and may luff as high as you please but you must give A room to keep clear. (Rule 16)

• Position 2: When A luffs to break the overlap, and then bears away to re-establish an overlap, you lose your luffing rights. You must immediately bear away to your proper course (or lower). If to sail your proper course you need to gybe, then you must gybe. (Rule 17.1)

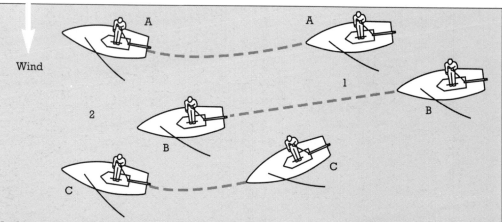

In this scenario, B establishes an overlap from clear astern to leeward of A, then while still overlapped with A, B gets an overlap to windward of C.

You are A:
• You are under no obligation to anticipate B getting an overlap, but when he does you must keep clear. Even if B does not luff, you will have to luff to avoid him running into your boom. (Rules 12 & 11)

You are B:
• Before you get an overlap you must keep clear. (Rule 11)

• When you first get an overlap to leeward of A, you must give him room to keep clear. Then you may sail up to your proper course, but no higher. (Rule 16)

• Your proper course is the course that keeps clear of C. (Definition of 'Proper Course')

• If C luffs, you must keep clear of C who has luffing rights over both you and A, because you both established overlaps on C's windward side. (Rule 11)

You are C:
• You have luffing rights over both A and B, so may luff as high as you like, but you must give them room to keep clear. (Rule 16)

Passing obstructions

You are A:
• You are the windward boat so you must keep clear of B. (Rule 11)

• If B sails to leeward of the obstruction, you may also go to leeward only if that is a proper course for you. If you do go to leeward, B must give you room, but as soon as the obstruction has been passed, you must keep clear. (Rules 11, 17.2, 18.2(a))

You are B:
• If you have luffing rights, you may luff A at any time and obviously may go to windward of the obstruction. If you change course you must give A room to keep clear. (Rules 11 & 16)

• If you don't have luffing rights you may only pass to windward if that is a proper course for you. Both sides are sometimes proper courses. (Rule 17.1)

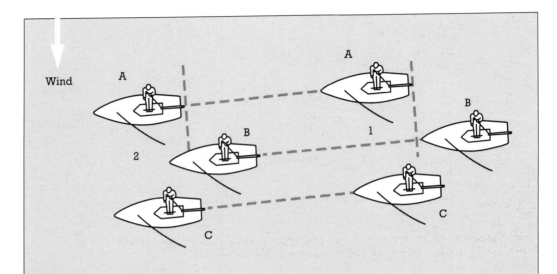

B is already overlapped with C when he gets an overlap to leeward of A.

You are B: C (the right-of-way boat) counts as a 'continuing obstruction'. When you first get the overlap between A and the continuing obstruction, was there sufficient room for you to pass between them? If you freeze the picture at position 2, and the answer is 'no', you have no right to establish the overlap. You should have sailed to leeward of C or to windward of A. (Rule 18.5)

• Whether or not you have luffing rights, if you choose to go to leeward, and B chooses to do likewise, you must give him room to pass between you and the obstruction. (Rule 18.2(a))

• If you both sail to leeward of the obstruction, once he has passed it, if you have luffing rights you may luff above your proper course, but you must give A room to keep clear. (Rule 16)

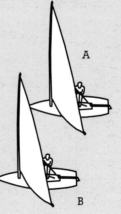

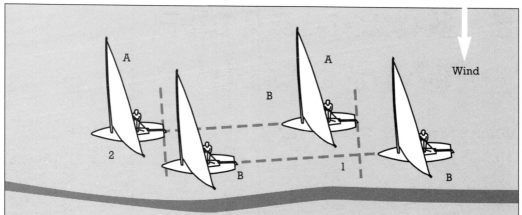

Continuing obstruction (e.g. river bank)

In position 1, B is about to get an overlap between A and the continuing obstruction.

Just as in the situation at the top of page 55, at the moment the overlap is established there is insufficient room for B to pass between A and the continuing obstruction, so B has no right to establish the overlap. (Rule 18.5)

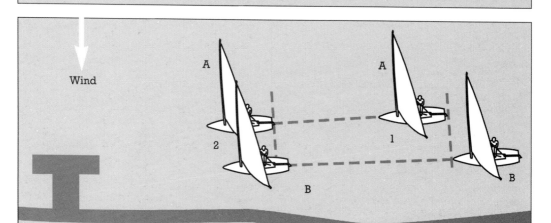

Continuing obstruction (e.g. river bank)

In position 1, B is about to get an overlap between A and the continuing obstruction.

Unlike the situation at the top of the page, at the moment the overlap is established there is sufficient room for B to pass between A and the continuing obstruction, so B has the right to establish the overlap. (Rule 18.5)

At position 2, A will need to give room to B, to allow B to get round the jetty. (Rules 18.5 & 18.2(a))

9 Rounding the Wing Mark

When the inside boat has to gybe to sail his proper course

Boat B has an undisputed overlap when the leading boat comes within two lengths. They will be gybing round the mark.

You are A:
• B has an overlap when you come within two lengths, and you are the give-way boat, so you must keep clear. (Rule 11)

• If you now get clear ahead, you must continue to keep clear until B has rounded the mark (that is, left it astern). You might do this by staying ahead, but if B is forced to alter course to avoid you before he has left the mark astern, you will have broken a rule. (Rule 18.2(a))

You are B:
• If you have luffing rights, (for example if you were more than two lengths away from A when you became overlapped) then as soon as you are 'about to round' the mark (which is usually about three boat lengths), you must sail no higher than your proper course. (Rule 17.1)

• As your proper course in this diagram is to gybe, and A is overlapped outside you, you must gybe no later than you would have done had A not been there. (If it's very windy and you want to do a loop and tack instead of gybing, you will have to slow down and let A go ahead). (Rule 18.4)

• After you have both gybed round the mark, and the mark is 'passed' (left clear astern with no chance of hitting it), then if you are overlapped, you will be the windward boat, and you must keep clear of A. A will have luffing rights. (Rule 11)

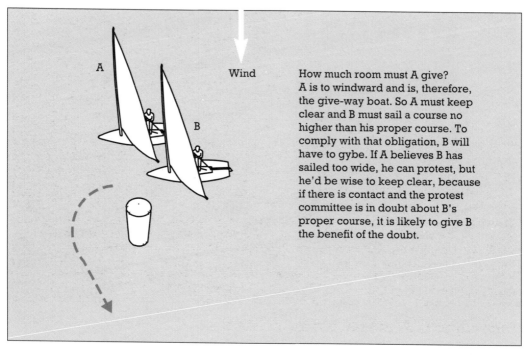

How much room must A give? A is to windward and is, therefore, the give-way boat. So A must keep clear and B must sail a course no higher than his proper course. To comply with that obligation, B will have to gybe. If A believes B has sailed too wide, he can protest, but he'd be wise to keep clear, because if there is contact and the protest committee is in doubt about B's proper course, it is likely to give B the benefit of the doubt.

When the inside boat does not have to gybe to sail his proper course

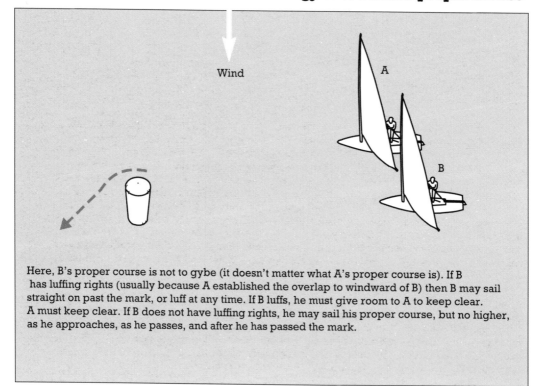

Here, B's proper course is not to gybe (it doesn't matter what A's proper course is). If B has luffing rights (usually because A established the overlap to windward of B) then B may sail straight on past the mark, or luff at any time. If B luffs, he must give room to A to keep clear. A must keep clear. If B does not have luffing rights, he may sail his proper course, but no higher, as he approaches, as he passes, and after he has passed the mark.

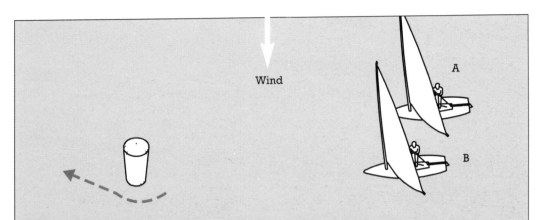

Here A, the give-way boat, will be on the inside. As soon as the boats are 'about to pass' the mark, B must start giving room, whether or not he has luffing rights. Room is 'the space a boat needs in the existing conditions when manoeuvring promptly in a seamanlike way'.

When the mark is passed (left astern with no risk of hitting it), B may return to his proper course, or if he has luffing rights, may sail as high as he likes, but must give A room to keep clear.

When there is doubt about the overlap

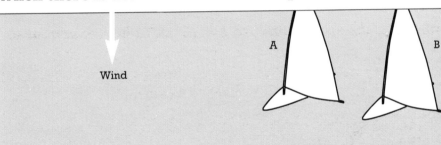

Often there is doubt whether or not there is an overlap at that critical moment when the leading boat gets to be two lengths from the mark. It is easy to draw a picture in a book, or place models carefully on the protest room table, but in real life the moment passes in an instant. If you are flying a spinnaker and you're preparing for a gybe you'll be reluctant to spare anyone to go to the bow or stern to see if there's an overlap. Then there is the difficulty of judging when the leading boat is two lengths from the mark. Before you know it, the moment is gone, and the boats are conerging towards the mark with the crews shouting 'no room' and 'water', usually mixed with a fair number of unprintable words and phrases to give emphasis to their opinion that the inside boat has or hasn't the right to room.

In this diagram, who can say without the use of measuring instruments whether B has an overlap, and whether A is two lengths from the mark? If A luffs a little at the critical moment as he is just about to get to two boat lengths, maybe he could break an overlap. If this was happening on the water with boats that are moving rather than being frozen in a picture, and the overlap is in doubt, then the answer to the question 'must A allow B to pass inside?' depends on what was happening before they got to this position: see the next two diagrams.

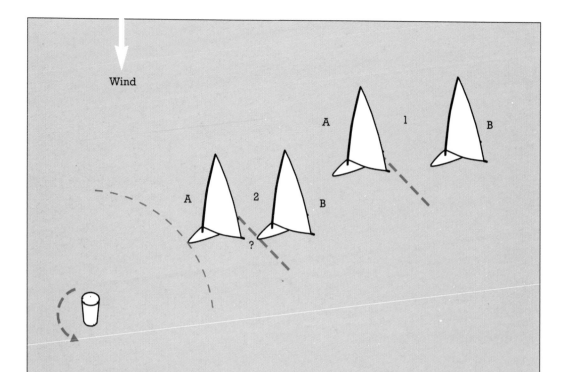

At position 1 there is no doubt that the boats are not overlapped. So when there is doubt at position 2, it is resolved in A's favour. If B surges forward on a wave, A should keep clear and protest. If the water is flat, A could hail something like 'no water' and hold his proper course for the mark. B would be wise to slow down and follow A. There is no obligation on A to give room just because B is claiming he has the right to room. On the other hand, both boats are, of course, required to try to avoid contact.

You are A:

Unless it is obvious that there is no overlap and B will not get one, try to get B's agreement that you are clear ahead well before your bow reaches the 'circle'. At least hail 'no overlap' well before you get to the critical 'two-lengths' position. If B subsequently claims that he got an inside overlap, the onus will be on him to establish that it was made in proper time.

The hail does not in itself place any obligation on B but will usually avoid a disagreement, a protest and, maybe, serious damage.

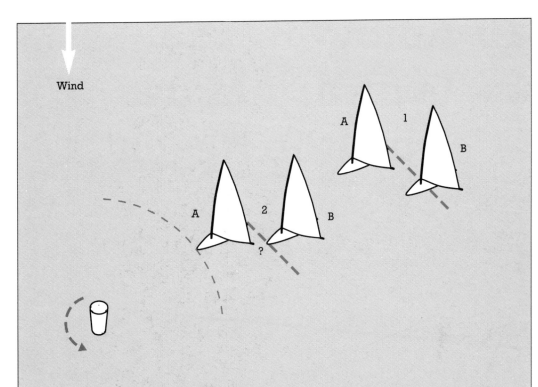

Here, at position 1 there is no doubt that the boats are overlapped. So when there is doubt at position 2, it is resolved in B's favour. Even if A surges forward on a wave and gets clear ahead at around two lengths, A must keep clear. Both boats are, of course, required to try to avoid contact

You are B:

Unless it is obvious that there is an overlap and A will not draw ahead and break it, try to get A's agreement that you have an overlap well before you reach the critical two-boat-lengths circle. At least hail 'overlap' before you get to the 'two-lengths' position. If A claims that he subsequently broke the overlap, the onus will be on him to establish that he did so before the two boat-lengths distance.

The hail does not in itself place any obligation on A, but will usually avoid a disagreement, a protest, and maybe damage.

10 Rounding the Leeward Mark from the Reach

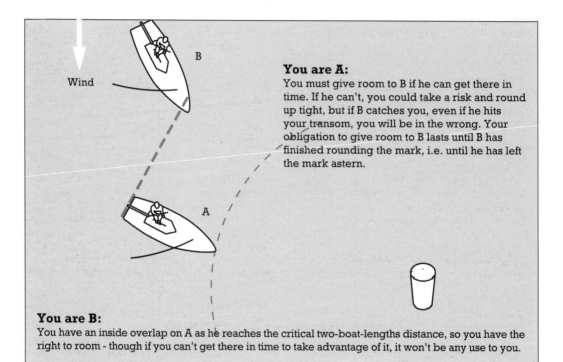

Wind

B

A

You are A:
You must give room to B if he can get there in time. If he can't, you could take a risk and round up tight, but if B catches you, even if he hits your transom, you will be in the wrong. Your obligation to give room to B lasts until B has finished rounding the mark, i.e. until he has left the mark astern.

You are B:
You have an inside overlap on A as he reaches the critical two-boat-lengths distance, so you have the right to room - though if you can't get there in time to take advantage of it, it won't be any use to you.

You are A:
- At position 1, you're not 'about to round' the mark, so:
  - If you have luffing rights you may luff and take B to windward of the mark if you want to, but if you change course you must give him room to keep clear, and if you reach a position where you are about to pass the mark (probably three boatlengths from the mark, could be more, and very rarely less than two), then you must immediately give room if B is still overlapped. (Rules 16, 18.1 & 18.2(a))
  - If you don't have luffing rights, you must not sail above your proper course to the mark. (Rule 17.1)

- Whether or not you have luffing rights, when you reach a point at which you are 'about to pass the mark' (about position 2) you must ignore your proper course and begin to bear away if necessary to give room. This is often more than two lengths from the mark. (Rules 18.1 & 18.2(a))

- Room is the 'space a boat needs in the existing conditions while manoeuvring promptly in a seamanlike way'. This usually means you will have to begin to bear away before you get to the critical

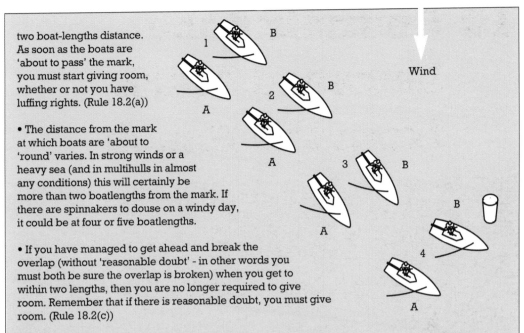

two boat-lengths distance. As soon as the boats are 'about to pass' the mark, you must start giving room, whether or not you have luffing rights. (Rule 18.2(a))

• The distance from the mark at which boats are 'about to 'round' varies. In strong winds or a heavy sea (and in multihulls in almost any conditions) this will certainly be more than two boatlengths from the mark. If there are spinnakers to douse on a windy day, it could be at four or five boatlengths.

• If you have managed to get ahead and break the overlap (without 'reasonable doubt' - in other words you must both be sure the overlap is broken) when you get to within two lengths, then you are no longer required to give room. Remember that if there is reasonable doubt, you must give room. (Rule 18.2(c))

• From a tactical point of view, it may be better to slow down, let B go ahead, and tighten up round the mark immediately behind B, to prevent yourself getting trapped down to leeward of him as you come away from the mark. However, bear in mind that once B breaks the overlap, he is no longer limited to rounding in a 'seamanlike manner', and may sail wide and come up hard on the mark.

• If you are still overlapped when the mark is passed (left astern with no risk of hitting it), you may return to your proper course or, if you have luffing rights, may sail as high as you like, but must give B room to keep clear. (Rule 16)

You are B:
• As you approach the mark, your obligation is to keep clear of A. (Rule 11)

• If A has luffing rights, he may luff you to windward of the mark, but he must stay outside a distance in which either of you would be 'about to round' the mark. (Rule 18.1)

• When you are 'about to round' the mark, you have the right to room to round inside A. Although 'room' does not mean that you can sail the course you might like to sail in the absence of A (what might be called a 'tactical' rounding) don't be intimidated by A trying to squeeze you right to the mark. If there is doubt in a protest, it is likely that A would be found not to have given sufficient room. If he doesn't give you enough room, it makes no difference whether you collide with the mark or the boat; whatever you hit (or if you hit both or even neither), if you feel you weren't given sufficient room, protest and sail on. (Rules 18.2(a), 28.1 & 31.3)

• Although A must give room, you remain the give-way boat, and when you have passed the mark (left it astern), A may luff to close-hauled (or his proper course if the next leg is a reach) and if he has luffing rights (can you remember how the overlap was established on the last leg?), A may luff and you must keep clear. (Rule 11)

When there is doubt about the overlap
See pages 60 and 61. The same principles apply here.

11 On the Run

All of Chapter 8 (On the Reach) applies equally on the run, but there are some additional situations which relate to boats on opposite tacks, and when one or both gybe.

You are A:
You are on opposite tacks and you are on port tack so your obligation is simple: to keep clear of B. (Rule 10)

You are B:
You have the right to sail where you like (your proper course is irrelevant) but if you change course you must give A room to keep clear. (Rule 16)

You are A:
You have the right to sail where you like (your proper course is irrelevant) but if you change course you must give B room to keep clear. (Rule 16)

You are B:
Your obligation is simple: to keep clear of A. If A is astern and going faster you must do something – you could gybe on to starboard tack and become the right-of-way boat, or move out of the way. (Rule 10)

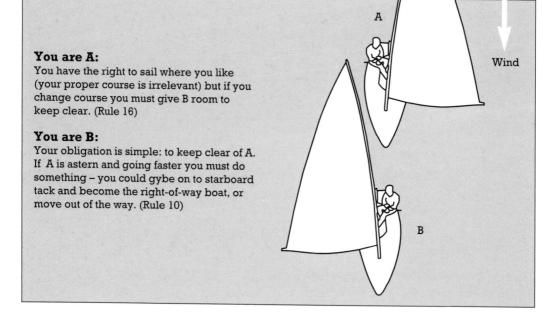

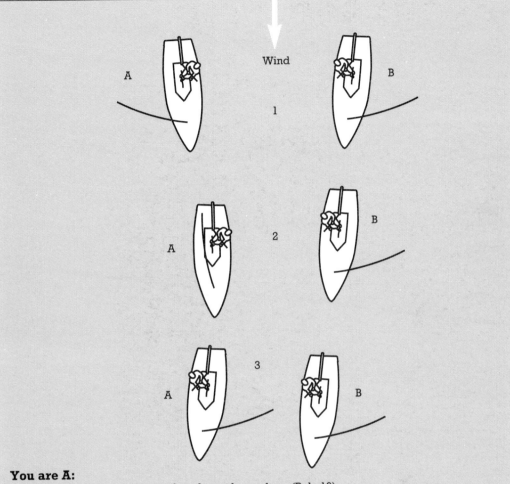

You are A:
• At position 1 you're on port tack and must keep clear. (Rule 10)

• At position 2 you are gybing into a 'give-way' position, and your obligation to keep clear continues. (Rule 11)

• At position 3 you are windward boat and still required to keep clear. (Rule 11)

You are B:
• In position 1 you are the right-of-way boat, and may sail any course, but if you change course you must give A room to keep clear. (Rules 10 and 16)

• While A is gybing at position 2, you continue to be right of way boat, but if you change course you must give A room to keep clear. (Rules 10, 11 and 16)

• You have luffing rights as soon as A's gybe is complete, so you may continue to sail any course, but if you change course you must give A room to keep clear. (Rules 11 and 16)

In short, you are the right of way boat throughout, but if you change course you must give A room to keep clear. (Rules 10, 11 and 16)

You are A:
• At position 1 you're the right-of-way boat and may luff up to your proper course. If you've got luffing rights, you may luff above your proper course.

• As soon as B's mainsail flips to fill on the port side (which means he's on starboard tack) you become the give-way boat and if you are on a collision course, as you are in position 2, you must do something to keep clear. (Rule 10)

You are B:
• At position 1 you are windward boat so you must keep clear. (Rule 11).

• From the moment you gybe you become the right-of-way boat, but if you alter course you must give A room to keep clear. (Rule 16)

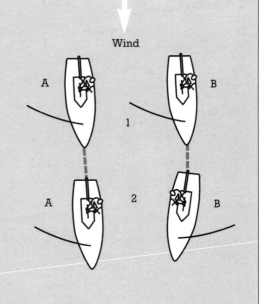

You are A:
• In position 1 you are the right-of-way boat, and may sail up to your proper course if you don't have luffing rights, and above your proper course if you do, but if you change course you must give B room to keep clear. (Rules 11 and 16)

• At position 2 you have gybed without changing course and you continue to be the right-of-way boat. As you did not change course you are not required to give B room to keep clear, but as I explained in Chapter 1, everyone must avoid contact if reasonably possible, so if your boom is going to make contact with B's boom, you should restrain it and protest. However, if there is contact with no damage, you cannot be penalised.

You are B:
• At position 1 you're to windward and must keep clear. (Rule 11)

• At position 1 it is wise to leave sufficient room for A to gybe, because if he does, you'll continue to be the give-way boat. (Rule 10)

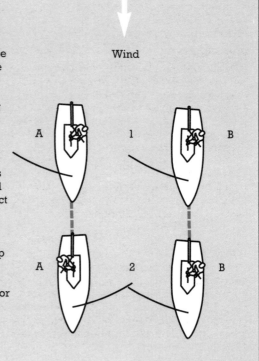

You are A:
• At position 1 you're the right-of-way boat, but if you change course you must give B room to keep clear. (Rules 10 & 16)

• At position 2 when B gybes you become the give-way boat and must keep clear. (Rule 11)

You are B:
• In position 1 you are the give-way boat, and must keep clear. (Rule 10)

• At position 2, when you gybe, you become the right-of-way boat, but A doesn't have to anticipate your being there, and there must be room for him to keep clear when you complete your gybe. (Rule 15)

• You may sail any course (you have luffing rights) but if you change course, you must give A room to keep clear. (Rule 16)

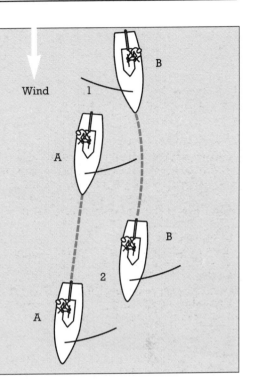

Passing a continuing obstruction

You are A:
• You are on starbord tack, and B is on port tack, and you are gaining on him, but because of the obstruction you can't force B to get out of your way as you could in open water.

• You must allow B to run along at a safe distance (for him) along the shore.

• However, if there is sufficient space between B and the shore for you to pass in safety at the moment you get an inside overlap, then you may sail between B and the shore. (Rule 18.5)

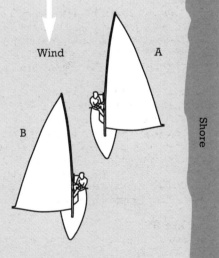

You are B:
• If there is insufficient room between you and the shore for A to 'pass in safety', then A, who is on starboard tack, must not run into your stern or poke his bow in between you and the shore.

• If there is sufficient room to sail through at the moment A gets the overlap (A might draw less than you) then he has the right to go in between you and the continuous obstruction. (Rule 18.5)

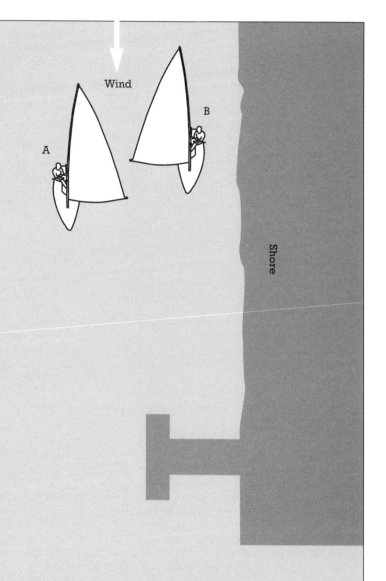

You are A:
• Your proper course is irrelevant. You may alter course towards B, but only in such a way that B is able to keep clear. (Rule 16)

• Once B cannot, with safety, get any closer to the shore, then you must give him room to sail along between you and the shore. (Rule 18.5)

• If something sticks out from the shore ahead of B, you'll have to sail out to give B room to pass round it. (Rule 18.5)

• If B gybes, you become the windward boat and must keep clear. (Rule 11)

You are B:
• You must keep clear. When you cannot safely get any closer to the shore, then you may sail along the shoreline (or, more exactly, along the line that is safely close to the shore); A must give you room to do that. (Rule 18.5)

• There is no requirement to hail if you think he is pushing you too close for safety, but there is no other way he is to know that you think things are getting unsafe, so hail for room when you need it.

• If there is a danger projecting from the shore ahead (or if you think there is) A must give you room to come out round it; again it is advisable, though not essential, to hail for room. (Rule 18.5)

• If you gybe, you become the right-of-way boat with luffing rights so you may luff above your proper course if you want to, but if you do you must give A room to clear. (Rules 11 and 16)

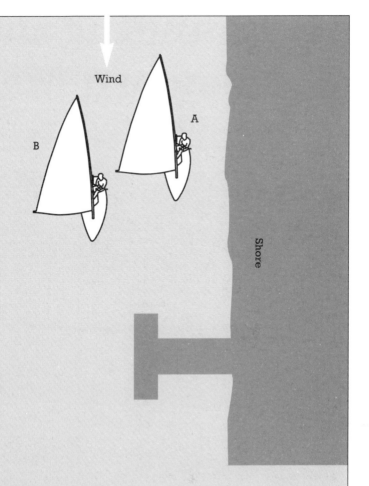

Wind

B

A

Shore

You are A:

• You must keep clear. When you cannot safely get any closer to the shore, then you may sail along the shoreline (or, more exactly, along the line that is safely close to the shore); B must give you room to do that. (Rule 18.5)

• There is no requirement to hail if you think he is pushing you too close for safety, but there is no other way he is to know that you think things are getting unsafe, so hail for room when you need it.

• If there is a danger projecting from the shore ahead (or if you think there is) B must give you room to come out round it; again it is advisable though not essential to hail for room.

You are B:

• If you have luffing rights and A is some distance from the shore or obstruction, you may luff, but you must give him room to keep clear. (Rules 11 and 16)

• When the shore (or other obstruction) obstructs A's ability to respond then you must stop luffing and bear away as is necessary to give him room. If he needs more room to come out round a projection, then you must give him room to do so. (Rule 18.5)

• If you don't have luffing rights, you may luff (in such a way that A can keep clear), up to your proper course. If your proper course is close to the shore, then you may force A towards the shore but must give A room when he gets there, as described in the last paragraph. (Rule 18.5)

12 Rounding the Leeward Mark from the Run

When the mark is a long way off, A, on port tack, would have to keep clear of B on starboard tack. On the other hand, if they were close to the mark, A has the right to room to round the mark. The mark-rounding rules come into effect when the boats are 'about to round' the mark. Under normal conditions, boats will have reached the 'about to round' position at two lengths at the latest. When boats are lowering spinnakers in windy conditions with a tidal stream under them, they may be 'about to round' at six or more boat lengths. On a river when boats are hardly making way against an adverse current, they may not be about to round till they less than one length from the mark.

At position 1, the boats are just reaching that critical position when they may be 'about to round' the mark:

You are A:
• At position 1, you are on port tack so you must keep clear. In this situation you have little choice but to gybe. If you think you are about to round, it would be best to shout this claim to B as he approaches. If he doesn't begin to give you room, keep clear and protest.
(Rules 10 & 18.1)

• At position 2 when you complete your gybe you are overlapped, so B has luffing rights, and you must keep clear. If you are not 'about to round', he can sail you as far as he likes the wrong side of the mark. If you are 'about to round the mark' then B must give you room.
(Rules 18.1 & 11)

• If you break the overlap (you could luff a little at position 2) then you become the right-of-way boat, but you can't just gybe in front of B, because as soon as you bear away you'll establish an overlap and be windward boat. (Rule 11)

• If after luffing to break the overlap at position 2, you bear away so that B is overlapped again, he doesn't have luffing rights and must not sail higher than his proper course. He will have to bear away and gybe if necessary to sail his proper course. (Rule 17.1)

• If either of you get close enough to the mark that you are 'about to round' then B must give you room. (Rule 18.2(a))

You are B:

• Position 1: Not to begin to give room, when A is claiming room, leaves you open to protest and possible disqualification. If you are really going to take A the wrong side of the mark (rarely a good tactic when other boats are going to overtake you both), there has to be no doubt that you are not 'about to round the mark'. (Rule 18.1)

• If A is in no doubt that you are not 'about to round' the mark, then you may sail any course, but if you change course you must give A room to keep clear. (Rule 10)

• If A gybes at position 2, nothing changes. If A is in no doubt that you are not 'about to round' the mark, then you may sail any course, but if you change course you must give A room to keep clear. (Rule 11)

• If the overlap is broken at position 3 you become the give-way boat, but you may sail any course. (Rule 12)

• If the overlap is re-established, although you are the right-of-way boat, you must sail no higher than your proper course, gybing if necessary. (Rule 17.1)

Now let's go back to the approach, and assume the boats are about to round the mark.

Wind

You are A:

• At position 1, you are overlapping on the inside. Even though you have not yet reached the two-lengths 'circle', B may have to start giving you room. (Rule 18.2(a))

• You must give B a chance to give you the room you need. This includes room to gybe (Rule 18.2(a))

• At position 3, even though you are the right-of-way boat with luffing rights, you may not sail B past the mark. You must gybe no later than the position at which you would have gybed to sail your proper course round the mark in the absence of B. (Rule 18.2(a)).

• When you have gybed, if you are still overlapped as you are in position 4, you become the give-way boat, so you must take no more room than that needed to round the mark in a seamanlike way. (Rule 18.2(a))

• When you have left the mark astern, then if you are still overlapped, you must keep clear. B has luffing rights and may sail higher than his close-hauled course. (Rule 18.2(a))

You are B:

• Position 1: Because A has an overlap as you become 'about to round' the mark, you may have to start giving room before you reach the two boatlength 'circle'. In this diagram, you will need to gybe at position 1. (Rule 18.2(a))

• After gybing at position 2, you become the give-way boat and you must keep clear. (Rule 11)

• A must not sail above his proper course, so at position 4 he must gybe. If he doesn't, you may protest, but you should still keep clear. (Rule 11)

• When A gybes at position 4, and you gybe, you become the right-of-way boat with luffing rights, but you must give room to A to round the mark in a seamanlike way. If he takes too much room, it is best to give it to him and protest. Then you can't lose the protest; if the protest committee finds he took too much room, he'll be disqualified, and if it finds he didn't, neither boat will be penalised. (Rule 18.2(a))

• Soon after position 4, it is best to drop astern and round up tight to the mark, rather than be left in A's windshadow. However, if you are still overlapped when A has completed his rounding (that is, left the mark astern), then as you have luffing rights, you may luff above close-hauled, but you must give A room to keep clear. (Rule 16)

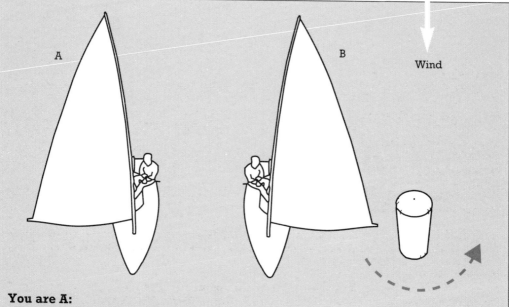

You are A:
• You must keep clear of B. (Rule 10)

• B must not sail above his proper course, so he must gybe. If he doesn't, it's best to continue to keep clear, and protest. (Rule 18.4)

You are B:
• Until you were 'about to round the mark', you could sail where you liked, but if you changed course you had to give him room to keep clear. (Rule 16)

• Now you are 'about to round the mark' you must sail no higher than your proper course. This will mean gybing of course (you can't sail straight on even though you are on starboard tack and A is on port tack). (Rule 18.4)

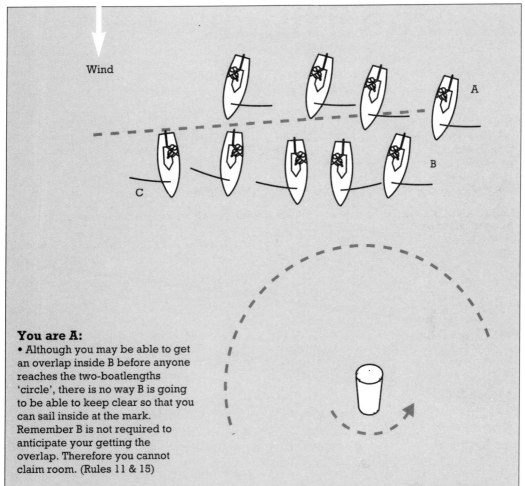

Wind

You are A:
• Although you may be able to get an overlap inside B before anyone reaches the two-boatlengths 'circle', there is no way B is going to be able to keep clear so that you can sail inside at the mark. Remember B is not required to anticipate your getting the overlap. Therefore you cannot claim room. (Rules 11 & 15)

• You do have an overlap, without doubt, on the inside of C and, unlike B, C is able to give room. C therefore must keep clear if you maintain the overlap to the 'circle'. (Rules 18.2(a) & 10)

You are B:
• As you've had the overlap for some time, those boats outside must keep clear (either because they are to windward on the same tack, or are on port tack). They might need to start giving you room before the two-length 'circle'. It might be a good idea to tell A that's it' too late to get an overlap now, and tell the boats outside you that they need to start giving you room now. (Rules 18.2(a))

• If they don't give you room, try to get the correct side of the mark, even if it means colliding with the mark or even the boat outside you (in which case you must protest, and you need not take a penalty for colliding with the mark or the other boat). (Rule 31.3)

You are C:
• This is not a good place to be! A has an inside overlap, and you are able to keep clear, so keep clear you must, as well as giving room to all the boats inside you. Next time, don't get into this position! (Rules 10 & 18.2(a))

13 The Finish

You finish when any part of your hull, crew or equipment first touches the finishing line, from the direction of the last mark. Typically, the first part of the boat to cross the line is the stem, but your crew's hand held over his head when he's out on the trapeze would count if that was his 'normal position'.

With a downwind finish, the spinnaker is usually the first piece of equipment to cross the line. If the spinnaker head was let out a few centimetres, and the boat often sailed with it like that, that would be OK, but a spinnaker with its head let go several metres would not count, because it would not be in its normal position (whether this had been done intentionally or not). A boat that had let its spinnaker go would be finished on the first piece of the boat to cross the line that was not out of position - probably its stem or pulpit.

You are 'racing' until you have cleared the finishing line and the finishing marks. You have cleared the line when no part of your boat or its equipment is straddling the line. You have

cleared the finishing marks when you are first in a position that is not in danger of making contact with a mark. The usual way of doing this is just to keep sailing right over the line near the middle (which would mean you are clear of the marks) or, if you finish near an end, to sail right through the line and get clear of the mark.

You don't have to cross the line completely; having finished with the first part of the boat or its equipment touching the line, you can duck back on to course side of the line if you want to.

When you have finished and cleared the line, you are still subject to the racing rules, but you cannot be penalised for infringing a 'when boats meet' rule (unless you interfere with a boat that is still racing). (Rules Part 2 Preamble and 22.1)

If you have not sailed the correct course, once you have finished you cannot go back and complete the course, because as soon as you have finished and cleared the line and marks, you are no longer 'racing'.

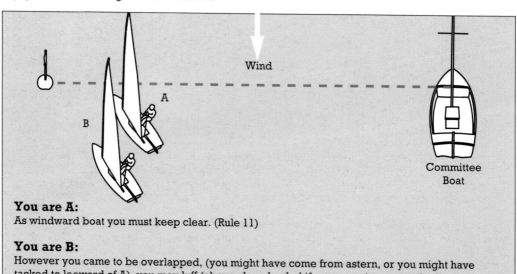

Wind

Committee
Boat

You are A:
As windward boat you must keep clear. (Rule 11)

You are B:
However you came to be overlapped, (you might have come from astern, or you might have tacked to leeward of A), you may luff (above close-hauled if necessary) to get to the line as quickly as you can without touching the mark, but if you luff you must give A room to keep clear. (Rule 16)

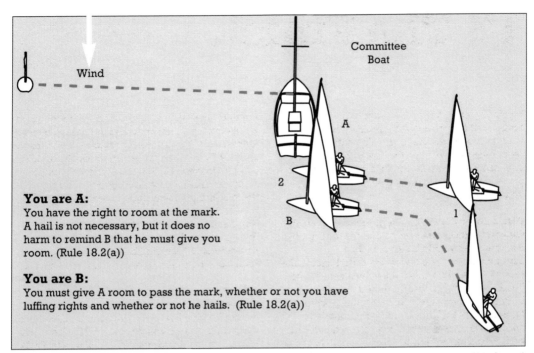

You are A:
You have the right to room at the mark. A hail is not necessary, but it does no harm to remind B that he must give you room. (Rule 18.2(a))

You are B:
You must give A room to pass the mark, whether or not you have luffing rights and whether or not he hails. (Rule 18.2(a))

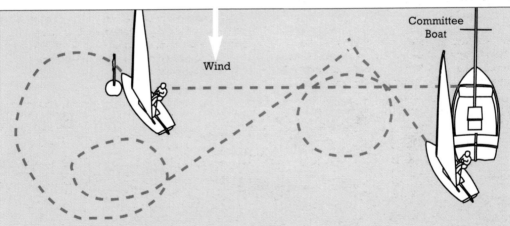

If, before finishing (or after finishing but before clearing the line and the finishing marks), you touch either finishing mark (it doesn't make any difference whether it's a buoy or the committee boat) you must sail clear of other boats and do a 360 penalty including a tack and a gybe (it doesn't matter which comes first). (Rule 31.2)

If you hit the mark after finishing but before clearing the line and the mark, you 'unfinish' yourself when you hit it. You must sail clear of other boats and do a 360 and then finish again. (Rule 31.2)

You don't have to be clear of the line when you do the 360 (you can be straddling it or on the post-finish side of it), but if having taken the penalty you are not on the pre-course side, you must go back to the pre-course side, and then finish. (Rule 31.2)

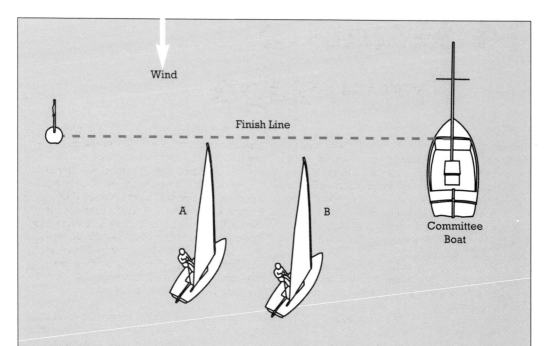

You are A:

As windward boat you must keep clear of B, even if B luffs. Whether or not he has luffing rights, B has the right to luff to head-to-wind to finish as quickly as he can. (Rule 11)

If B hails for room to tack, you have to make a quick judgement as to whether you can fetch the committee boat on this tack. To 'fetch' means to pass without tacking, so you can luff to head-to-wind but you must get past the bow of the committee boat without going through head-to-wind. If you can, you can refuse room (you should hail a refusal such as "no room") but if you refuse room and then cannot fetch the committee boat, you'll have to do a 720 degree penalty before you can be recorded as having finished. (Rule 19)

If you cannot lay the committee boat, you must either:

1. Tack, or

2. Hail back 'you tack' and take on the responsibility of giving room to B (typically by ducking B's stern as he tacks).

You are B:

Because of the obstruction ahead, you may hail A for room to tack. If A returns a hail indicating a refusal, you may 'shoot' the line; that is go head-to-wind and hope you will have sufficient way for your bow to touch the line - that's all you need! If A hails a refusal and then fails to fetch the committee boat without tacking, you may protest him if he doesn't take a penalty. (Rule 19)

If A responds to your hail by tacking, you must tack as soon as possible. (Rule 19.1(a))

If A responds to your hail by hailing 'you tack', you must tack. (Rule 19.1(b))

14 Means of Propulsion

You must not 'increase, maintain or decrease' the speed of your boat by any other means than by using 'wind and water'. At some dinghy championships more than half of the disqualification's are for infringing the 'propulsion' rule. Most, if not all, of the protests are put in by vigilant juries aware of the huge unfair advantage that can be gained. Indeed, the differential in speed between a dinghy complying with the propulsion rule and one propelled illegally by a skilled crew paying no attention to it can, in very light winds, be so enormous that in a half-knot zephyr the complying boat wouldn't have reached the windward mark when the infringing boat had completed a triangle, a sausage, and a beat, travelling six times as fast. (Rule 42)

The difference lessens as the windspeed increases, but can still be significant in a competitive fleet at a windspeed of 15 knots. Since the differences in boat speed between top competitors in competitive dinghy fleets is often as little as one tenth of one per cent, infringing Rule 42 is an obvious attraction not only to the unscrupulous, but to the honest sailor when he sees less honest sailors 'getting away with it'.

At major dinghy championships the sailing instructions often allow the jury to disqualify boats it sees infringing the propulsion rule, without a hearing. (Rule 67)

When the scoring system allows one or more race scores (your worst results) to be discarded in calculating a series score, then a disqualification for infringing the propulsion rule (Rule 42) cannot be discarded.

So what does Rule 42 seek to control? If you rock a rig to windward in still air, the sail passing through the still air has the same effect as moving air passing over a still sail: a driving force is set up. The same sort of effect, though not quite as effective, can be obtained by hauling in the sail: the force drives the boat forward, and the rig or sail can be returned to 'leeward' ready for another go. Waggling the tiller can also drive a hull through calm water. Moving the trunk of the body forward and backwards, even in strong winds, can flap the leech and increase the sail's drive.

With practice one can become very efficient at driving a boat through the water on a calm day; it's really quite fun, though very energetic. There is a minority of dinghy sailors who would prefer that there were no restrictions (i.e. Rule 42 was removed), and indeed in the appendix (B) for board sailing, Rule 42 is deleted. Removing the propulsion restrictions would certainly make life easier for race committees and juries, since the rule is not easy to enforce. However, the vast majority of good sailors do not want 'kinetics' (imparting energy from moving crew weight into forward motion) to be part of sailing. Attitudes might change; up to a few years ago, board sailors did not want to allow kinetics, now they do, resulting in only very fit and strong people being able to win championships.

At championships, and at well-organised regional regattas, a jury goes afloat to look for offenders; a good race committee will also not hesitate to take action. However, this should not alter your policy; if you see someone pumping, rocking or sculling, you should protest (displaying a protest flag and hailing in the usual way).

15 Taking a Penalty

When and where to take a penalty

When you know you've broken a rule or a sailing instruction, you must take a penalty or retire promptly from the race, unless the rule or sailing instruction broken is one which requires you do something while racing, and you were not racing at the time of the incident (i.e. it occurred before the preparatory signal or after you finish and clear the finishing line). In such a case you do not have to take a penalty (but if you've caused damage you will have to pay for the repair).

If you are racing and you break a 'when boats meet' rule, you must take a 720 penalty promptly. Let's suppose you are sailing up the first beat, and you are close-hauled on port tack, chatting to your crew about tactics. Suddenly you are aware of a starboard tack boat bearing away under your stern. As he bears away under your stern he shouts something at you so you know he is aggrieved. What should you do? Tell him you're going to take a penalty, and immediately sail clear and do a 720. Actually, if he doesn't hail "protest" and display a protest flag, he cannot protest, but that should not affect whether or not you take the penalty. If you know you have infringed, and the other guy is aggrieved, the paragraph called 'Sportsmanship and the Rules' at the beginning of the rule book make it clear that you must take the penalty. Not to do so could be cause to bring a Rule 69 hearing against you for a 'gross breach of good sportsmanship'.

What if you did see him coming and when you were just about to tack, he shouted "carry on"? You carry on on port tack and he bears away under your stern. Should you take a penalty? No. By accepting his invitation to carry on, and him ducking your stern, you have in fact kept clear. (By the way, the hail of 'carry on' did not compel you to sail on; you could have tacked if you had wanted to).

What if he bears away under your stern, but says nothing. My recommendation is that if he shows no signs of being aggrieved, then you can assume you kept clear, but bear in mind that a protest against you lodged by a third yacht witnessing the incident might succeed, but if the protestor is within hailing distance he has to hail to you that he's going to protest, in which case you can take your penalty if you think you've broken a rule.

If you touch a mark while racing, then you are honour-bound to take a 360 degree penalty, even if no-one saw you. This is the test of a good sportsman. We all need to be good sportsmen if we are going to play this great game of fleet racing without the need for referees or judges.

If you sail the wrong course, or propel the boat by means other than by the use of 'wind and water', or you are on the course side of the starting line at the starting signal, you cannot exonerate yourself by taking a penalty. However, you can often exonerate yourself by doing something else; if you realise before you finish that you've sailed the wrong course you can go and sail the right one (if you can do it within the time limit!); if you've gone round a mark the wrong way, you can unwind yourself and go round it the right away; if you were a premature starter you can usually go back and start; but having pumped your way down the reaching leg, or paddled, or moored up to the shore for an ice-cream, or - heaven forbid - failed to rescue someone in distress, then there is no exoneration procedure open to you, and you must retire from the race immediately you realise you have broken the rule or sailing instruction.

Remember that if you want to take a 720 penalty after an incident in the preparatory period, or you hit a starting mark in the preparatory period, then you may (in fact you must) take the penalty as soon as you can, so if the infringement is some minutes before the start, you will not be disadvantaged.

If the infringement happens on or close to the finishing line, then you must do the 720 as soon as possible (on either side of the finishing line or its extensions), and then cross the finishing line in the direction from the last mark. It is possible, therefore, to finish (when the first part of the boat touches the line), then break a rule of Part 2 before clearing the line (which has the effect of 'unfinishing'), do a 720, then come back wholly behind the line and 'refinish' when the first part of the boat touches the line again from the course side.

If you break a 'when boats meet' rule (for example by taking room at a mark to which you are not entitled) and you hit the mark, you can exonerate yourself by doing just a 720; you don't have to do the 360 for hitting the mark as well. If you have broken more than one rule in an incident, you need take only one 720 penalty.

How to take the penalty

The standard penalty for infringing a 'when boats meet' rule is the '720 degree turn', which is described in Rule 44. If there is nothing said about penalties in the sailing instructions, then the 720 penalty applies.

If you have room, do the penalty immediately (and it costs you nothing to tell the other guy you're going to do it). If there isn't room, tell the other guy you're going to do it, immediately sail to where there is room, or slow down to let the surrounding boats pass. Rotate your boat through two turns. Do the second turn immediately after the first and, make sure you finish pointing in the same direction that you were when you started the turns (if you're on a beat make sure you're not 90 degrees short). Make sure you include two tacks and two gybes. When you are training, you should practise doings 720's so that you can do them as quickly as possible; there's no point in adding to the penalising effect by getting into irons. When you

practise 720's you'll realise that when you're on a beat, it's usually best to bear off first rather than tack. (Rule 44.2)

Sometimes sailing instructions replace the '720' penalty with a 'scoring' penalty system (usually for keelboat events in which it is thought unsafe for boats to be doing circles). When the sailing instructions prescribe a 'scoring penalty' then instead of doing a 720, you must display a yellow flag and tell the race committee after the finish. (Rule 44.3)

Protest or take a penalty?

After the preparatory signal, if you are involved in an incident with another boat (or several other boats) in which you think a rule has, or may have, been broken, you have to make a decision and you have to make it quickly. If there has been a collision, however small or unavoidable, then there must have been an infringement and of course even without a collision there might have been an infringement.

If you know you have broken a rule but think the other boat has broken one too, you can protest and take a penalty. Hail "protest", display a red flag, then sail clear and take the penalty.

If you have a collision, but were in the right or entitled to room, and there is no damage then you cannot be penalised. You can sail on. If there is damage (to either boat) which you could have avoided (though you need not act to avoid contact until it is clear that the other boat is not keeping clear or giving room), then you can do a 720 penalty to exonerate yourself. If the damage is serious, then you cannot exonerate yourself with a 720, and you must retire.

16 Protesting

Some people, even top competitors, say they find protesting unpleasant. Protesting need not be done with any acrimony whatsoever, and unless we want to evolve a breed of referees to blow whistles and penalise on the spot (and there'll need to be lots of them all over the course, because under such a system no one will dream of taking a penalty if they don't hear a whistle) then we have to accept that the sport is policed by the following system:

When a competitor knows he has infringed a rule he takes a penalty (or retires).

When a competitor thinks another competitor has infringed a rule, and the other competitor doesn't retire or take a penalty, he protests.

When the race committee (or jury if there is one) sees a rule infringement which affects the fairness of the competition and the boat doesn't take a penalty, it protests.

In my opinion (though many judges will not agree with me) there is one other consideration that affects a decision as to whether or not a penalty should be taken or a protest made against another boat when a rule is broken. That is, whether or not the right-of-way boat (or the boat with the right to room) is aggrieved. You're on starboard tack a lap ahead of a beginner on port tack and you have to duck under his stern. There is nothing to be gained by protesting; a word over a beer after the race would be much more appropriate. Of course in this scenario there is no rule requiring you to protest. But what if you're the one on port tack and a rival ducks under your stern, but says nothing. As I said in the last chapter, I believe if he is not aggrieved, you can assume there's no infringement. That's the criteria I use when I'm racing. If he says even 'tut tut', I'll do a penalty if I think I've infringed. Sometimes I'm not sure if I have infringed. If the other guy thinks I have, that's usually enough for me, and I'll go and do my turns.

When you consider another boat has broken a rule and you feel aggrieved about it, you will want to protest. This chapter is about how to lodge a protest.

There are certain requirements that must be met before a protest can be accepted as valid, and a hearing opened. The only requirements you actually need to remember are those which have to be met out there on the water; the rest you can look up in this book* when you are back at the clubhouse.

Things to remember on the water

Any boat may protest, provided that the boat was involved in or witnessed an incident. Even if you have been involved in a previous incident in which you will be disqualified (after a hearing), that doesn't remove your right to protest about a later incident. (ISAF Case 2)

The first thing you need to do is hail the word "protest". The rule says this must be done 'at the first reasonable opportunity'. So there is time to ask him whether he's going to take a penalty, and if he says 'no', hail 'protest' and display your flag. If you get no reaction to the hail, it's best to repeat it more loudly.

The next thing you need to do is display a protest flag, and this too must be done 'at the first reasonable opportunity'. Don't wait too long. Many protests have been found to be invalid because the flag was not displayed within thirty seconds. The flag must be red. It doesn't matter what the shape is, but it must be red, and it must be a flag, not a red glove or waterproof jacket. The usual flag is the code flag B which has swallow tails, but a rectangular red flag will do just as well. It must be displayed conspicuously which means it mustn't be too small, and it must be up in the rigging and not lying on the deck. It must be kept displayed until you finish, or if the incident is near the finishing line, until the race committee

---

*   or better still, 'Protests & Appeals' published by Fernhurst Books.

acknowledges seeing the flag (you can draw the committee's attention to it after finishing).

There used to be a provision for single-handers not to have to keep it displayed, but that has gone now, so if you sail a single-handed boat, I recommend you fix some gadget like a flag in a 35mm film canister tied to your vang, so that a quick pull on the rope tail springs the flag, and it is clearly visible for the rest of the race without your having to worry about it.

If the flag is already being displayed because of a previous incident, then that's fine, you don't have to pull it down and put it up again, or display another one.

The purpose of the hail and the flag is two-fold. It gives an opportunity for him to take a penalty, and if he decides not to take a penalty, then it marks the moment so that he can remember what happened.

Remember, you cannot protest if you don't hail and display a red flag, but you don't have to go ahead and lodge the protest if you have hailed and displayed a red flag.

Whatever level you race at, even if you think you will never want to protest, I recommend you ensure that a red flag is included in your racing kit.

If the other man might not have heard your hail of "protest" at the time of the incident you should inform him again at the next opportunity you get, even if the next opportunity is ashore.

Things to do when you come ashore

You need to fill in a protest form. If you can't find one, and unless there is some special sailing instruction (ugh!) any bit of paper will do provided that you include certain pieces of vital information. Most people make too much of filling in the form. By including too much detail, you're more likely to do yourself harm than good, and you'll certainly wear out the brain unnecessarily. Initially you need only identify the incident, but as you will need to include your identity (you are the protestor), and that of the protestee, the number of the rule broken, you may as well complete that initially if you can.

You need to lodge the form with the protest committee within the time limit (which is two hours after the last boat finishes unless otherwise specified in the sailing instructions). If there is a good reason for any delay, the protest committee must extend the time limit. (Rule: 61.3)

Preparing your witnesses

If there is someone who you think saw the incident, approach him and, having simply identified the incident so that he knows what you're taking about, ask him what he saw. Don't tell him anything and don't ask leading questions. If you think what he saw is what you believe really happened, then ask him if he will be a witness at the hearing.

At the hearing, when you are invited to call witnesses, explain to the chairman that you have not discussed the case with your witness, you merely asked what he saw and considered that as this was more or less what actually happened, you thought he would be a good witness. When your witness gives his evidence and is questioned, it will invariably become obvious to the protest committee that he has in no way been influenced, and his credibility and the value of his evidence will help you enormously. You'd do better with no witness at all than a 'coached' witness; their complicity is obvious to all but the most inexperienced protest committee.

Conducting yourself at the hearing

If you are an experienced racing skipper sailing in a minor event, there is a good chance that you will know more about the rules and procedures than the protest committee does. Use this knowledge carefully if you wish not to be disadvantaged. At any hearing you should treat the committee members (and indeed the other parties and witnesses) with respect. They are usually fellow sailors doing their best to be fair, but even when this is not the case, losing your cool gains you nothing.

The procedure

Appendix P of the racing rules, which gives a recommended procedure for protest committees, is very well written and easy to follow. Here is a summary.

The protestor and protestee are called to the hearing. You must both be present during all of the taking of evidence (from each of you, and of any witnesses called by you, of your opponent or of the protest committee).

The validity of the protest must be considered by the protest committee:

Was a hail of 'Protest' made, and was it made at the first reasonable opportunity after the incident?
Was the protest flag displayed, and was it displayed at the first reasonable opportunity after the incident? Was it conspicuously displayed? Was it kept displayed till the finish?

Was the written protest received in proper time?

Did the written protest identify the nature of the incident?

Although the protest committee must extend the time limit for receiving protests if there is a good reason for a delay, it has no power to excuse any of the other requirements, and if they are not met the protest must be found to be invalid, and refused. If the protest is ruled as valid, the protest committee must proceed to the next stage: the hearing of evidence.

The protestor describes his version of the incident; the protestee then does likewise. Each may question the other and the protest committee members may question both. Each is invited to call witnesses, one at a time, and each witness describes his version of the incident, and is questioned by the parties (the protestor and the protestee) and the committee. The committee may call witnesses, or the committee members may themselves be witnesses in which case they give their evidence and may be questioned. The protestor summarises his case; the protestee summarises his defence.

The protest committee deliberates in private (if there were observers, they too are asked to leave) and produces 'facts found' (what it thinks happened), its decision and the grounds for that decision. The parties are then recalled and the chairman reads out the details.

17 Requesting Redress & Appealing

If you think your position in a race, or in a series, has been made significantly worse through no fault of your own, you can sometimes successfully 'request redress' (often erroneously called 'protesting the race committee'). Redress is usually in the form of points which the protest committee considers you would have been awarded had you finished without being prejudiced. (Rules: 62, 64.2)

Unlike a protest (for which there are several validity requirements), it is rare for a request for redress to be refused on the grounds it is invalid. The only reason for refusal to hear a redress request would be that it was received after the closing time for receiving protests, (or two hours after the incident) without a good reason.

You can write your request on any bit of paper, but is usual to use a protest form even though many of the prompts are not relevant. For example, you don't have to display a protest flag, or have made a hail.

So it is not difficult to get a hearing; being awarded redress is another matter! Very generally the procedure at the hearing is the same as a protest hearing, except that if you are the only one requesting redress, you will take on the 'protestor's' role, and a representative of the race committee will usually act as the 'defendant'. The protest committee itself should be independent of the race committee. If the event is anything more than a club race, wise organisers will have appointed a jury independent of the race committee; at an international event there'll usually be an international jury.

At club events the usual practice is for the race committee to arrange a protest committee as independent as is practical, if a request for redress is received by the race committee.

Like a protest hearing, there are the same distinct parts to the hearing: the taking of evidence (from you, your fellow redress requesters if there are any, the race committee, and anyone else you or the protest committee see fit to call); the assessment by the protest committee (sitting in private) as to whether redress is applicable; and lastly, if redress is applicable, what redress will be given.

Redress can only be given to you when:

• Your finishing position has been made significantly worse.

• You've done nothing wrong yourself. So if you were disqualified for being over the line at the start, and are simply complaining that there were some boats ahead of you that were not disqualified, you can't get redress. (You could protest the guilty boats, of course.)

• Your finishing position was affected for one of the following reasons:

(a) The race committee (or the protest committee) made an improper action or omission. So if some passing whale rammed you, you cannot get redress; a rescue boat would be another matter, as that is under the control of the race committee. If the race committee fails to make a signal correctly and this affected you, you'd be entitled to redress. The race committee is not permitted to prejudice anyone's finishing position (in a race or series of races), whether or not it adheres to the rules and sailing instructions which govern its conduct.

For example, if the race committee writes itself a sailing instruction saying it can shorten course at any time for any reason, and it shortens course for no apparent reason just as your rival approaches the first mark after twenty minutes of racing - his father is the race officer - you would have a legitimate claim for redress (though the only redress might be to re-sail the race). Conversely, if the sailing instructions said the first leg would be 3 kilometres long and it was only 2.5, it would be impossible to argue that any competitor had been prejudiced and so no redress could be given.

(b) You have been physically damaged by a boat required to keep clear or give room or by a vessel not racing that was required to keep clear of you (for example under the collision regulations). So if you're on starboard and a boat on port rams you, putting a hole in your side, and you have to retire, you can get redress. You can only get redress if you're damaged; if you simply got tangled up with this port tacker while some close rivals pass you, you cannot get redress. If at a mark you are entitled to room but not given it and forced the wrong side, you must return to round the mark correctly, and although you may successfully protest the boat that didn't give you room, you are not entitled to redress for the fifty places you may have lost, because you were not physically damaged.

(c) You went to help someone in distress. Since if you seen someone in distress, you must go to their aid, it's only fair that if you lose places by your heroic act you are then awarded redress.

(d) You have been significantly affected by someone who is penalised (under rule 69) for cheating, or infringing the 'Fair Sailing' rule.

The protest committee will hear your evidence and that of your witnesses, and if relevant the evidence and advice of the race committee. In private it will then 'find facts' and assess whether these facts meet the criteria for giving redress, and if they do, what redress is to be given.

If your request meets the above criteria, then you must be given redress. It is not unusual to be awarded points equal to a position the protest committee thinks you would have achieved had you not been prejudiced, or points equal to your 'average to date in the series' (perhaps not counting your 'discard'). In giving redress, the only restriction imposed on the protest committee is that its decision shall be as equitable as possible to all boats affected. Faced with a complex situation, a protest committee may decide that the most equitable arrangement is 'no adjustment in finishing positions'. To abandon or cancel a race is rarely the most equitable solution, although sometimes there is no alternative. (Rule: 64.2)

Appealing

If you are penalised as a result of a hearing, you usually have the right to appeal against the protest committee's decision, but to be eligible you need to be a 'party' directly affected by the decision against which you are appealing. (Rule: 77, 78)

If you are indirectly affected, for instance, if you find yourself in a lower position as a result of the protest committee giving redress to another boat then you must first request redress on the grounds that the committee's action materially prejudiced your finishing position, and if you are not satisfied with that decision, you may appeal. You may also appeal against a decision not to hear your protest or your request for redress, or against the fairness of redress awarded as a result of your request.

Sometimes there is no right to appeal. You have no right to appeal:

• When, at an international event, an 'international jury' has been appointed, and it complies with the requirements of Appendix Q; or

• When 'it is essential to determine promptly the result of a race that will qualify a boat to compete in a later stage of an event'. In the UK, the approval from the Royal Yachting Association is also required. In the USA, no approval is required from the USSA. In all cases, the fact that decisions are not open to appeal must be announced in the notice of the race and in the sailing instructions. (Rule: Appendix M 1.2(11)

Unless the facts found by the protest committee are completely incompatible with all the evidence or with the protest committee's own diagram, you can appeal solely on a question of interpretation of the rules, and not against the facts found by the protest committee. (Rule: 70.1)

The protest committee may itself refer a case it has decided for confirmation or correction. (Rule: 70.1(b))

How to appeal

This varies from country to country, so look at Rule 70 and any prescription to the rule which your own National Authority may have written.

The 1997–2000 Rules

Sportsmanship and the Rules

Competitors in the sport of sailing are governed by a body of rules that they are expected to follow and enforce. A fundamental principle of sportsmanship is that when competitors break a rule they will promptly take a penalty or retire.

Introduction

The Racing Rules of Sailing includes two main sections. The first, Parts 1–7, contains rules that affect all competitors. The second section contains appendices that provide details of rules, rules that apply to particular kinds of racing, and rules that affect only a small number of competitors or officials.

The racing rules are revised and published every four years by the International Sailing Federation (ISAF), the international authority for the sport. This edition becomes effective on 1 April 1997. No changes are contemplated before 2001, but changes determined by the ISAF to be urgent will be made as needed and announced through national authorities.

Terminology A term used in the sense stated in the Definitions is printed in italics or, in preambles, in bold italics (for example, *racing* and **racing**). Other words and terms are used in the sense ordinarily understood in nautical or general use. 'Race committee' includes any person or committee performing a race committee function. 'Class rules' includes rules of handicapping and rating systems.

Appendices When the rules of an appendix apply, they take precedence over any conflicting rules in Parts 1–7. A reference to a rule of an appendix will contain the letter of the appendix and the rule number; for example, 'rule A1.1'. (There is no Appendix I or Appendix O.)

Changes to the Rules The prescriptions of a national authority, class rules or the sailing instructions may change a racing rule only as permitted in rule 86.

PART 1 – FUNDAMENTAL RULES

1 SAFETY

1.1 Helping Those in Danger
A boat or competitor shall give all possible help to any person or vessel in danger.

1.2 Life-saving Equipment and Personal Buoyancy
A boat shall carry adequate life-saving equipment for all persons on board, including one item ready for immediate use, unless her class rules make some other provision. Each competitor is individually responsible for wearing personal buoyancy adequate for the conditions.

2 FAIR SAILING
A boat and her owner shall compete in compliance with recognized principles of sportsmanship and fair play. A boat may be penalized under this rule only if it is clearly established that these principles have been violated.

3 ACCEPTANCE OF THE RULES
By participating in a race conducted under these racing rules, each competitor and boat owner agrees
(a) to be governed by the *rules*;
(b) to accept the penalties imposed and other action taken under the *rules*, subject to the appeal and review procedures provided in them, as the final determination of any matter arising under the rules; and
(c) with respect to such determination, not to resort to any court or other tribunal not provided by the *rules*.

4 DECISION TO RACE
A boat is solely responsible for deciding whether or not to *start* or to continue *racing*.

5 DRUGS
A competitor shall neither take a substance nor use a method banned by Appendix L. An alleged breach of this rule shall not be grounds for a *protest*, and rule 63.1 does not apply.

PART 2 – WHEN BOATS MEET

The rules of Part 2 apply between boats that are sailing in or near the racing area and intend to **race**, *are* **racing**, *or have been* **racing** *However, a boat not* **racing** *shall not be penalized for breaking one of these rules, except rule 22.1. The International Regulations for Preventing Collisions at Sea or government right-of-way rules apply between a boat sailing under these rules and a vessel that is not, and they replace these rules if the sailing instructions so state.*

Section A – Right of Way

A boat has right of way when another boat is required to **keep clear** *of her. However, some rules in Sections B and C limit the actions of a right-of-way boat.*

10 ON OPPOSITE TACKS
When boats are on opposite *tacks*, a *port-tack* boat shall *keep clear* of a *starboard-tack* boat.

11 ON THE SAME TACK, OVERLAPPED
When boats are on the same *tack* and *overlapped*, a *windward* boat shall keep clear of a *leeward* boat.

12 ON THE SAME TACK, NOT OVERLAPPED
When boats are on the same *tack* and not overlapped, a boat *clear astern* shall *keep clear* of a boat *clear ahead*.

13 WHILE TACKING
After a boat passes head to wind, she shall *keep clear* of other boats until she is on a close-hauled course. During that time rules 10, 11 and 12 do not apply. If two boats are subject to this rule at the same time, the one on the other's port side shall *keep clear*.

Section B – General Limitations

14 AVOIDING CONTACT
A boat shall avoid contact with another boat if reasonably possible. However, a right-of-way boat or one entitled to *room*
(a) need not act to avoid contact until it is clear that the other boat is not *keeping clear* or giving *room*, and
(b) shall not be penalized unless there is contact that causes damage.

15 ACQUIRING RIGHT OF WAY
When a boat acquires right of way, she shall initially give the other boat *room* to *keep clear*, unless she acquires right of way because of the other boat's actions.

16 CHANGING COURSE
When a right-of-way boat changes course, she shall give the other boat *room* to *keep clear*.

17 ON THE SAME TACK; PROPER COURSE
17.1 A boat that establishes a *leeward overlap* from *clear astern* within two of her hull lengths of a *windward* boat shall not sail above her *proper course* during that *overlap* while the boats are less than that distance apart, unless as a result she becomes *clear astern*.

17.2 Except on a beat to windward, while a boat is less than two of her hull lengths from a *leeward* boat or a boat *clear astern* steering a course to *leeward* of her, she shall not sail below her *proper course* unless she gybes.

Section C – At Marks and Obstructions

When a Section C rule applies, the rules in Sections A and B continue to apply unless the Section C rule modifies them or states that they do not apply.

18 PASSING MARKS AND OBSTRUCTIONS
18.1 When this Rule Applies
Rule 18 applies at a *mark* or *obstruction* to be left on the same side when boats are about to pass it until they have passed it. However, it does not apply

(a) at a starting *mark* or its anchor line surrounded by navigable water from the time the boats are approaching them to start until they have passed them, or
(b) between boats on opposite *tacks* when they are on a beat to windward or when the *proper course* for one of them to pass the *mark* or *obstruction* is to tack.

18.2 Giving Room; Keeping Clear
(a) When boats are *overlapped* before one of them reaches the *two-length zone*, if the outside boat has right of way she shall give the inside boat *room* to pass the *mark* or *obstruction*, or if the inside boat has right of way the outside boat shall *keep clear*. If they are still *overlapped* when one of them reaches the *two-length zone*, the outside boat's obligation continues even if the *overlap* is broken later. This rule does not apply if the outside boat is unable to give *room* when the *overlap* begins.
(b) If a boat is *clear ahead* when she reaches the *two-length zone*, the boat *clear astern* shall *keep clear* even if an *overlap* is established later. Rule 10 does not apply. If the boat *clear ahead* tacks, rule 13 applies and this rule no longer does.
(c) If there is reasonable doubt that a boat established or broke an *overlap* in time, it shall be presumed that she did not.

18.3 Tacking
If two boats were on opposite *tacks* and one of them tacked within the *two-length zone* to pass a *mark* or *obstruction*, rule 18.2 does not apply. The boat that tacked
(a) shall not cause the other boat to sail above close-hauled to avoid her or prevent the other boat from passing the *mark* or *obstruction*, and
(b) shall *keep clear* if the other boat becomes overlapped inside her, in which case rule 15 does not apply.

18.4 Gybing
When rule 18.2(a) applies and an inside *overlapped* right-of-way boat must gybe at the *mark* or *obstruction* to sail her *proper course*, she shall pass no farther from the *mark* or *obstruction* than needed to sail that course.

18.5 Passing a Continuing Obstruction
At a continuing *obstruction*, rule 18.2 is modified so that while boats are passing the *obstruction* an outside boat's obligation ends if the *overlap* is broken, and a boat *clear astern* may establish an inside *overlap* provided there is *room* at that time to pass between the other boat and the *obstruction*. If she does so, her obligation under rule 18.2(b) ends.

19 ROOM TO TACK AT AN OBSTRUCTION
19.1 When safety requires a close-hauled boat to make a substantial course change to avoid an *obstruction* and she intends to tack, but cannot tack and avoid another boat on the same *tack*, she shall hail for *room* to do so. Before tacking she shall give the hailed boat time to respond. The hailed boat shall either
(a) tack as soon as possible, in which case the hailing boat shall also tack as soon as possible, or
(b) immediately reply 'You tack', in which case the hailing boat shall immediately tack and the hailed boat shall give *room*, and rules 10 and 13 do not apply.

19.2 Rule 19.1 does not apply at a starting *mark* or its anchor line surrounded by navigable water from the time boats are approaching them to *start* until they have passed them or at a *mark* that the hailed boat can fetch. When rule 19.1 applies, rule 18 does not.

Section D – Other Rules

When rule 20 or 21 applies between two boats, Section A rules do not.

20 STARTING ERRORS; PENALTY TURNS; MOVING ASTERN
A boat sailing towards the pre-start side of the starting line or its extensions to comply with rule 29.1 or rule 30.1 shall *keep clear* of a boat not doing so until she is completely on the pre-start side. A boat making penalty turns shall *keep clear* of one that is not. A boat moving astern by backing a sail shall *keep clear* of one that is not.

21 CAPSIZED, ANCHORED OR AGROUND; RESCUING
If possible, a boat shall avoid a boat that is capsized or has not regained control after capsizing, is anchored or aground, or is trying to help a person or vessel in danger. A boat is capsized when her masthead is in the water.

22 INTERFERING WITH ANOTHER BOAT
22.1 If reasonably possible, a boat not *racing* shall not interfere with a boat that is *racing*.

22.2 A boat shall not deliberately interfere with a boat making penalty turns to delay her.

PART 3 – CONDUCT OF A RACE

25 SAILING INSTRUCTIONS AND SIGNALS
Sailing instructions shall be made available to each boat before a race begins. The race committee shall conduct the race using the visual and sound signals defined in the Race Signals and any other signals included in the sailing instructions.

26 STARTING SYSTEMS 1 AND 2
26.1 A race shall be started by using either System 1 or System 2. Signals shall be made at five-minute intervals. Times shall be taken from the visual signals; the failure of a sound signal shall be disregarded. Signals shall be as follows (flags of a single colour may be replaced by shapes of the same colour):

Signal	System 1	System 2
Warning	Class flag; 1 sound	Yellow flag; 1 sound
Preparatory	Flag P; 1 sound	Blue flag; 1 sound
Starting	Flags removed; 1 sound	Red flag; 1 sound

26.2 In System 1, when classes are started at ten-minute intervals, the warning signal for each succeeding class shall be displayed at the starting signal of the preceding class. When five-minute intervals are used, flag P shall be left displayed until the last class starts and the warning signal for each succeeding class shall be displayed at the time of the preparatory signal of the preceding class. If there is a general recall, the warning and preparatory signals of any succeeding classes shall be removed immediately after the general recall has been signalled.

26.3 In System 2, each signal shall be removed one minute before the next is made. When classes are started at ten-minute intervals, the starting signal for each class shall be the warning signal for the next. When classes are started at five-minute intervals, the preparatory signal for each class shall be the warning signal for the next. When class flags are used, they shall be displayed before or with the preparatory signal for the class.

27 OTHER RACE COMMITTEE ACTIONS BEFORE THE STARTING SIGNAL
27.1 No later than the warning signal, the race committee shall signal or otherwise designate the course to be sailed if the sailing instructions have not stated the course, and it may replace one course signal with another, signal that a designated short course will be used (flag S), and apply rule 40 (flag Y).

27.2 No later than the preparatory signal, the race committee may move a starting *mark* and may apply rule 30.

27.3 Before the starting signal, the race committee may postpone (flag AP) or *abandon* the race (flag N over H or A) for any reason.

28 SAILING THE COURSE
28.1 A boat shall *start*, pass each *mark* on the required side in the correct order, and *finish*, so that a string representing her wake after starting and until *finishing* would, when drawn taut, lie on the required side of each *mark* and touch each rounding *mark*. She may correct any errors to comply with this rule, provided she has not already *finished*. After *finishing*, a boat need not cross the finishing line completely.

28.2 A *mark* has a required side for a boat only when she is on a leg that the *mark* begins, bounds or ends, except that a starting *mark* begins to have a required side when she is approaching the starting line from its pre-start side to *start*.

29 STARTING; RECALLS
29.1 On the Course Side at the Start
When at her starting signal any part of a boat's hull, crew or equipment is on the course side of the starting line, the boat shall sail completely to the pre-start side of the line before *starting*.

29.2 Individual Recall
When at her starting signal a boat must comply with rule 29.1 or rule 30.1, the race committee shall promptly display flag X. The signal shall be displayed until all such boats are completely on the pre-start side of

the starting line or its extensions and have complied with rule 30.1 if it applies, but not later than four minutes after the starting signal or one minute before any later starting signal, whichever is earlier.

29.3 General Recall

When at the starting signal several unidentified boats are on the course side of the starting line or there has been an error in the starting procedure, the race committee may signal a general recall (flag First Substitute). The preparatory signal for a new start for the recalled class shall be made one minute after the First Substitute is lowered, and the starts for any succeeding classes shall follow the new start.

30 STARTING PENALTIES

30.1 I Flag Rule

If flag I has been displayed before or with her preparatory signal, and any part of a boat's hull, crew or equipment is on the course side of the starting line or its extensions during the minute before her starting signal, she shall sail to the pre-start side of the line around either end before *starting*.

30.2 Z Flag Rule

If flag Z has been displayed before or with her preparatory signal, and any part of a boat's hull, crew or equipment is identified within the triangle formed by the ends of the starting line and the first mark during the minute before her starting signal and a general recall is then signalled, she shall, without a hearing, be given a 20% scoring penalty calculated as stated in rule 44.3(c). If the race is restarted, resailed or rescheduled, she shall still be given the penalty.

30.3 Black Flag Rule

If a black flag has been displayed before or with her preparatory signal, and any part of a boat's hull, crew or equipment is identified within the triangle formed by the ends of the starting line and the first *mark* during the minute before her starting signal, the boat will be disqualified without a hearing. If the race is restarted, resailed or rescheduled, she is not entitled to compete in it. If a general recall is signalled or the race is *abandoned*, the race committee shall display her sail number.

31 TOUCHING A MARK

31.1 While *racing*, a boat shall not touch a starting *mark* before *starting*, a *mark* that begins, bounds or ends the leg of the course on which she is sailing, or a finishing *mark* after *finishing*.

31.2 A boat that has broken rule 31.1 may, after getting well clear of other boats as soon as possible, take a penalty by promptly making one complete 360° turn including one tack and one gybe. When a boat takes the penalty after touching a finishing *mark*, she shall return completely to the course side of the line before *finishing*. However, if a boat has gained a significant advantage in the race or series by touching the *mark* she shall retire.

31.3 When a boat is wrongfully compelled by another boat to break rule 31.1, she shall be exonerated
(a) if the other boat acknowledges breaking a rule of Part 2 by taking a penalty or retiring immediately, or
(b) under rule 64.1(b), after successfully protesting another boat involved in the same incident.

32 SHORTENING OR ABANDONING AFTER THE START

After the starting signal, the race committee may *abandon* the race (flag N or flag N over H or A) or shorten the course (flag S), as appropriate,
(a) because of an error in the starting procedure,
(b) because of foul weather,
(c) because of insufficient wind making it unlikely that any boat will *finish* within the time limit,
(d) because a *mark* is missing or out of position, or
(e) for any other reason directly affecting the safety or fairness of the competition.
However, after one boat has sailed the course and *finished* within the time limit, if any, the race committee shall not *abandon* the race without considering the consequences for all boats in the race or series.

33 CHANGING THE COURSE AFTER THE START

At any rounding *mark* the race committee may signal a change of the direction of the next leg of the course by displaying flag C and the compass bearing of that leg before any boat begins it. The race committee may change the length of the next leg by displaying flag C and a '–' if the leg will be shortened or a '+' if the leg will be lengthened.

34 MARK MISSING

When a *mark* is missing or out of position, the race committee shall, if possible,
(a) replace it in its correct position, or
(b) substitute one of similar appearance, or a buoy or vessel displaying flag M.

35 TIME LIMIT

If one boat sails the course as required in rule 28.1 and *finishes* within the time limit, if any, all boats shall be scored unless the race is *abandoned*. If no boat *finishes* within the time limit, the race committee shall *abandon* the race.

36 RACES TO BE RESTARTED OR RESAILED

If a race is restarted or resailed, a breach of a *rule*, other than rule 30.3, in the original race shall not prohibit a boat from competing or, except under rule 30.2, 30.3 or 69, cause her to be penalized.

PART 4 – OTHER REQUIREMENTS WHEN RACING

*Part 4 rules apply only to boats **racing**.*

40 PERSONAL BUOYANCY

When flag Y is displayed before or with the warning signal, competitors shall wear life-jackets or other adequate personal buoyancy. Wet suits and dry suits are not adequate personal buoyancy.

41 OUTSIDE HELP

A boat may receive outside help as provided for in rule 1. Otherwise, she shall not receive help except for an ill or injured crew member or, after a collision, from the crew of the other boat.

42 PROPULSION

42.1 Basic Rule

Except when permitted in rule 42.3 or rule 45, a boat shall compete by using only the wind and water to increase, maintain or decrease her speed. Her crew may adjust the trim of sails and hull, and perform other acts of seamanship, but shall not otherwise move their bodies to propel the boat.

42.2 Prohibited Actions

Without limiting the application of rule 42.1, these actions are prohibited:
(a) pumping: repeated fanning of any sail either by trimming and releasing the sail or by vertical or athwartships body movement;
(b) rocking: repeated rolling of the boat, induced either by body movement or adjustment of the sails or centreboard, that does not facilitate steering;
(c) ooching: sudden forward body movement, stopped abruptly;
(d) sculling: repeated movement of the helm not necessary for steering;
(e) repeated tacks or gybes unrelated to changes in the wind or to tactical considerations.

42.3 Exceptions

(a) A boat's crew may move their bodies to exaggerate the rolling that facilitates steering the boat through a tack or a gybe, provided that, just after the tack or gybe is completed, the boat's speed is not greater than it would have been in the absence of the tack or gybe.
(b) Except on a beat to windward, when surfing (rapidly accelerating down the leeward side of a wave) or planing is possible, the boat's crew may pull the sheet and the guy controlling any sail in order to initiate surfing or planing, but only once for each wave or gust of wind.
(c) Any means of propulsion may be used to help a person or another vessel in danger.
(d) To get clear after grounding or colliding with another boat or object, a boat may use force applied by the crew of either boat and any equipment other than a propulsion engine.

43 COMPETITOR CLOTHING AND EQUIPMENT

43.1 (a) Competitors shall not wear or carry clothing or equipment for the purpose of increasing their weight.
(b) Furthermore, a competitor's clothing and equipment shall not weigh more than 8 kilograms, excluding a hiking or trapeze harness and clothing (including footwear) worn only below the knee. Class rules or sailing instructions may specify a lower weight or a higher weight up to 10 kilograms. Class rules may include footwear and other clothing worn below the knee within that weight. A hiking or trapeze harness shall have positive buoyancy and shall not weigh more than 2 kilograms, except that class rules may specify a higher weight up to 4 kilograms. Weights shall be determined as required by Appendix J.
(c) When a measurer in charge of weighing clothing and equipment believes a competitor may have broken rule 43.1(a) or rule 43.1(b) he shall report the matter in writing to the protest committee.

43.2 Rule 43.1(b) does not apply to boats required to be equipped with lifelines.

44 PENALTIES FOR BREAKING RULES OF PART 2

44.1 Taking a Penalty

A boat that may have broken a rule of Part 2 while *racing* may take a penalty at the time of the incident. Her penalty shall be a 720° Turns Penalty unless the sailing instructions specify the use of the Scoring Penalty or some other penalty. However, if she caused serious damage or gained a significant advantage in the race or series by her breach she shall retire.

44.2 720° Turns Penalty

After getting well clear of other boats as soon after the incident as possible, a boat takes a 720° Turns Penalty by promptly making two complete 360° turns (720°) in the same direction, including two tacks and two gybes. When a boat takes the penalty at or near the finishing line, she shall return completely to the course side of the line before *finishing*.

44.3 Scoring Penalty

(a) A boat takes a Scoring Penalty by displaying a yellow flag at the first reasonable opportunity after the incident, keeping it displayed until *finishing*, and calling the race committee's attention to it at the finishing line. At that time she shall also inform the race committee of the identity of the other boat involved in the incident. If this is impracticable, she shall do so at the first reasonable opportunity within the time limit for *protests*.

(b) If a boat displays a yellow flag, she shall also comply with the other parts of rule 44.3(a).

(c) The boat's penalty score shall be the score for the place worse than her actual finishing place by the number of places stated in the sailing instructions, except that she shall not be scored worse than Did Not Finish. When the sailing instructions do not state the number of places, the number shall be the whole number (rounding 0.5 upward) nearest to 20% of the number of boats entered. The scores of other boats shall not be changed; therefore two boats may receive the same score.

44.4 Limits on Penalties

(a) When a boat intends to take a penalty as provided in rule 44.1 and in the same incident has touched a *mark*, she need not take the penalty provided in rule 31.2.

(b) A boat that takes a penalty shall not be penalized further with respect to the same incident unless she failed to retire when rule 44.1 required her to do so.

45 HAULING OUT; MAKING FAST; ANCHORING

A boat shall be afloat and off moorings at her preparatory signal. Thereafter, she may not be hauled out or made fast except to bail out, reef sails, or make repairs. She may anchor or the crew may stand on the bottom. She shall recover the anchor before continuing in the race unless she is unable to do so.

46 PERSON IN CHARGE

A boat shall have on board a person in charge designated by the member or organization that entered the boat. See rule 75.

47 LIMITATIONS ON EQUIPMENT AND CREW

47.1 A boat shall use only the equipment on board at her preparatory signal.

47.2 No person on board shall leave, unless ill or injured or to help a person or vessel in danger. However, a person leaving the boat by accident or to swim shall be back on board before the boat continues in the race.

48 FOG SIGNALS AND LIGHTS

When safety requires, a boat shall sound fog signals and show lights as required by the International Regulations for Preventing Collisions at Sea or applicable government rules.

49 CREW POSITION

49.1 A boat shall use no device other than hiking straps to project a competitor's body outboard.

49.2 When lifelines are required by the class rules or the sailing instructions they shall be taut, and competitors shall not position any part of their torsos outside them, except briefly to perform a necessary task. On boats equipped with upper and lower lifelines of wire, a competitor sitting on the deck facing outboard with his waist inside the lower lifeline may have the upper part of his body outside the upper lifeline.

50 SETTING AND SHEETING SAILS

50.1 Changing Sails

When headsails or spinnakers are being changed, a replacing sail may be fully set and trimmed before the replaced sail is lowered. However, only one mainsail and, except when changing, only one spinnaker shall be carried set at a time.

50.2 Spinnaker Poles, Whisker Poles

Only one spinnaker pole or whisker pole shall be used at a time except when gybing. When in use, it shall be attached to the foremost mast.

50.3 Use of Outriggers

(a) No sail shall be sheeted over or through an outrigger, except as permitted in rule 50.3(b). An outrigger is any fitting or other device so placed that it could exert outward pressure on a sheet or sail at a point from which, with the boat upright, a vertical line would fall outside the hull or deck planking. For the purpose of this rule, bulwarks, rails and rubbing strakes are not part of the hull or deck planking and the following are not outriggers: a bowsprit used to secure the tack of a working sail, a bumkin used to sheet the boom of a working sail, or a boom of a boomed headsail that requires no adjustment when tacking.

(b) (1) Any sail may be sheeted to or led above a boom that is regularly used for a working sail and is permanently attached to the mast from which the head of the working sail is set.

(2) A headsail may be sheeted or attached at its clew to a spinnaker pole or whisker pole, provided that a spinnaker is not set.

50.4 Headsails

The difference between a headsail and a spinnaker is that the mid-girth of a headsail, measured from the mid-points of its luff and leech, does not exceed 50% of the length of its foot, and no other intermediate girth exceeds a percentage similarly proportional to its distance from the head of the sail. A sail tacked down behind the foremost mast is not a headsail.

51 MOVING BALLAST

All movable ballast shall be properly stowed, and water, dead weight or ballast shall not be moved for the purpose of changing trim or stability. Floorboards, bulkheads, doors, stairs and water tanks shall be left in place and all cabin fixtures kept on board.

52 MANUAL POWER

A boat's standing rigging, running rigging, spars and movable hull appendages shall be adjusted and operated only by manual power.

53 SKIN FRICTION

A boat shall not eject or release a substance, such as a polymer, or have specially textured surfaces that could improve the character of the flow of water inside the boundary layer.

54 FORESTAYS AND HEADSAIL TACKS

Forestays and headsail tacks, except those of spinnaker staysails when the boat is not close-hauled, shall be attached approximately on a boat's centre-line.

PART 5 – PROTESTS, HEARINGS, MISCONDUCT AND APPEALS

Section A – Protests

60 RIGHT TO PROTEST AND REQUEST REDRESS

60.1 A boat may

(a) protest another boat, but not for an alleged breach of a rule of Part 2 unless she was involved in or saw the incident; or

(b) request redress.

60.2 A race committee may

(a) protest a boat, but not as a result of a report by a competitor from another boat or other *interested party* or of information in an invalid *protest*;

(b) request the protest committee to consider giving redress; or

(c) report to the protest committee requesting action under rule 69.1(a).

60.3 A protest committee may

(a) protest a boat, but not as a result of a report by a competitor from another boat or other *interested party*, except under rule 61.1(c), nor as a result of information in an invalid *protest*;

(b) consider giving redress; or

(c) act under rule 69.1(a).

61 PROTEST REQUIREMENTS

61.1 Informing the Protestee

(a) A boat intending to protest because of an incident occurring in the racing area that she is aware of shall hail 'Protest' and conspicuously display a red flag at the first reasonable opportunity for each. She shall display the flag either until she *finishes* or retires, or, if the incident occurs near the finishing line, until the race committee acknowledges seeing her flag. In all other cases she shall inform the other boat as soon as reasonably possible.

(b) A race committee or protest committee intending to protest a boat under rule 60.2(a) or rule 60.3(a) because of an incident it observes in the racing area shall inform her after the race within the time limit determined by rule 61.3. In all other cases it shall inform her as soon as reasonably possible.

(c) During the hearing of a valid *protest*, if the protest committee decides to protest a boat that was involved in the incident but is not a *party* to that hearing, it shall inform the boat as soon as reasonably possible of its intention and of the time and place of the hearing.

61.2 Protest Contents

A *protest* shall be in writing and identify
(a) the protestor and protestee;
(b) the incident, including where and when it occurred;
(c) any *rule* the protestor believes was broken; and
(d) the name of the protestor's representative.
Provided the written *protest* identifies the incident, other details may be corrected before or during the hearing.

61.3 Protest Time Limit

A *protest* by a boat, or by the race committee or protest committee about an incident the committee observes in the racing area, shall be delivered to the race office no later than the time limit stated in the sailing instructions. If none is stated, the time limit is two hours after the last boat in the race *finishes*. Other race committee or protest committee *protests* shall be delivered to the race office within two hours after the committee receives the relevant information. The protest committee shall extend the time if there is good reason to do so.

62 REDRESS

62.1 A request for redress shall be based on a claim that a boat's finishing place in a race or series has, through no fault of her own, been made significantly worse by
(a) an improper action or omission of the race committee or protest committee,
(b) physical damage because of the action of a boat that was breaking a rule of Part 2 or of a vessel not *racing* that was required to keep clear,
(c) giving help (except to herself or her crew) in compliance with rule 1.1, or
(d) a boat against which a penalty has been imposed under rule 2 or disciplinary action has been taken under rule 69.1(b).

62.2 The request shall be made in writing within the time limit of rule 61.3 or within two hours of the relevant incident, whichever is later. No protest flag is required.

Section B – Hearings and Decisions

63 HEARINGS

63.1 Requirement for a Hearing

A boat or competitor shall not be penalized without a hearing, except as provided in rules 30.2, 30.3, 67 and A1.1. A decision on redress shall not be made without a hearing. The protest committee shall hear all *protests* that have been delivered to the race office unless it approves a protestor's request to withdraw the *protest*.

63.2 Time and Place of the Hearing

All *parties* to the hearing shall be notified of the time and place of the hearing, the *protest* or redress information shall be made available to them, and they shall be allowed reasonable time to prepare for the hearing.

63.3 Right to Be Present

(a) The *parties* to the hearing, or a representative of each, have the right to be present throughout the hearing of all the evidence. When the *protest* claims a breach of a rule of Part 2, Part 3 or Part 4, the representatives of boats shall have been on board at the time of the incident, unless there is good reason for the protest committee to rule otherwise. Any witness, other than a member of the protest committee, shall be excluded except when giving evidence.

(b) If a *party* to the hearing does not come to the hearing, the protest committee may nevertheless decide the *protest*. If the *party* was unavoidably absent, the committee may reopen the hearing.

63.4 Interested Party

A member of a protest committee who is an *interested party* shall not take any further part in the hearing but may appear as a witness. A *party* to the hearing who believes a member of the protest committee is an *interested party* shall object as soon as possible.

63.5 Validity of the Protest

At the beginning of the hearing the protest committee shall decide whether all requirements for the *protest* have been met, after first taking any evidence it considers necessary. If all requirements have been met, the *protest* is valid and the hearing shall be continued. If not, it shall be closed.

63.6 Taking Evidence and Finding Facts

The protest committee shall take the evidence of the *parties* to the hearing and of their witnesses and other evidence it considers necessary. A member of the protest committee who saw the incident may give evidence. A *party* to the hearing may question any person who gives evidence. The committee shall then find the facts and base its decision on them.

63.7 Protests Between Boats in Different Races

A *protest* between boats sailing in different races conducted by different organizing authorities shall be heard by a protest committee acceptable to those authorities.

64 PROTEST DECISIONS

64.1 Penalties and Exoneration

(a) When the protest committee decides that a boat that is a *party* to the hearing has broken a *rule*, she shall be disqualified unless some other penalty applies. A penalty shall be imposed whether or not the applicable *rule* was mentioned in the *protest*.

(b) When as a consequence of breaking a *rule* a boat has compelled another boat to break a *rule*, rule 64.1(a) does not apply to the other boat and she shall be exonerated.

(c) If a boat has broken a *rule* when not *racing*, her penalty shall apply to the race sailed nearest in time to that of the incident.

64.2 Decisions on Redress

When the protest committee decides that a boat is entitled to redress under rule 62, it shall make as fair an arrangement as possible for all boats affected, whether or not they asked for redress. This may be to adjust the scoring (see rule A4 for some examples) or finishing times of boats, to *abandon* the race, to let the results stand or to make some other arrangement. When in doubt about the facts or probable results of any arrangement for the race or series, especially before *abandoning* the race, the protest committee shall take evidence from appropriate sources.

64.3 Decisions on Measurement Protests

(a) When the protest committee finds that deviations in excess of tolerances specified in the class rules were caused by damage or normal wear and do not improve the performance of the boat, it shall not penalize her. However, the boat shall not *race* again until the deviations have been corrected, except when the protest committee decides there is or has been no reasonable opportunity to do so.

(b) When the protest committee is in doubt about the meaning of a measurement rule, it shall refer its questions, together with the relevant facts, to an authority responsible for interpreting the rule. In making its decision, the committee shall be bound by the reply of the authority.

(c) When a boat disqualified under a measurement rule states in writing that she intends to appeal, she may compete in subsequent races without changes to the boat, but will be disqualified if she fails to appeal or the appeal is decided against her.

(d) Measurement costs arising from a *protest* involving a measurement rule shall be paid by the unsuccessful *party* unless the protest committee decides otherwise.

65 INFORMING THE PARTIES AND OTHERS

65.1 After making its decision, the protest committee shall promptly inform the *parties* to the hearing of the facts found, the applicable *rules*, the decision, the reasons for it, and any penalties imposed or redress given.

65.2 A *party* to the hearing is entitled to receive the above information in writing, provided she asks for it in writing from the protest committee within seven days of being informed of the decision. The committee shall then promptly provide the information, including, when relevant, a diagram of the incident prepared or endorsed by the committee.

65.3 When the protest committee penalizes a boat under a measurement rule, it shall send the above information to the relevant measurement authorities.

66 REOPENING A HEARING

The protest committee may reopen a hearing when it decides that it may have made a significant error, or when significant new evidence becomes available within a reasonable time. It shall reopen a hearing when required by the national authority under rule F5. A *party* to the hearing may ask for a reopening no later than 24 hours after being informed of the decision. When a hearing is reopened, a majority of the members of the protest committee shall, if possible, be members of the original protest committee.

67 RULE 42 AND HEARING REQUIREMENT

When so stated in the sailing instructions, the protest committee may penalize without a hearing a boat that has broken rule 42, provided that a member of the committee or its designated observer has seen the incident. A boat so penalized shall be informed by notification in the race results.

68 DAMAGES

The question of damages arising from a breach of any *rule* shall be governed by the prescriptions, if any, of the national authority.

Section C – Gross Misconduct

69 ALLEGATIONS OF GROSS MISCONDUCT

69.1 Action by a Protest Committee

(a) When a protest committee, from its own observation or a report received, believes that a competitor may have committed a gross breach of a *rule* or of good manners or sportsmanship, or may have brought the sport into disrepute, it may call a hearing. The protest committee shall promptly inform the competitor in writing of the alleged misconduct and of the time and place of the hearing.
(b) A protest committee of at least three members shall conduct the hearing, following rules 63.2, 63.3, 63.4 and 63.6. If it decides that the competitor committed the alleged misconduct it shall either
(1) warn the competitor or
(2) impose a penalty by excluding the competitor, and a boat when appropriate, from a race, or the remaining races of a series or the entire series, or by taking other action within its jurisdiction.
(c) The protest committee shall promptly report a penalty, but not a warning, to the national authorities of the venue, of the competitor and of the boat owner.
(d) If the competitor has left the venue and cannot be notified or fails to attend the hearing, the protest committee shall collect all available evidence and, when the allegation seems justified, make a report to the relevant national authorities.
(e) When the protest committee has left the event and a report alleging misconduct is received, the race committee or organizing authority may appoint a new protest committee to proceed under this rule.

69.2 Action by a National Authority

(a) When a national authority receives a report required in rule 69.1(c) or rule 69.1(d), or a report alleging a gross breach of a *rule* or of good manners or sportsmanship or conduct that brought the sport into disrepute, it may conduct an investigation and, when appropriate, shall conduct a hearing. It may then take any disciplinary action within its jurisdiction it considers appropriate against the competitor or boat, or other person involved, including suspending eligibility, permanently or for a specified period of time, to compete in any event held within its jurisdiction, and suspending ISAF eligibility under rule K3.1(a).
(b) The national authority of a competitor shall also suspend the ISAF eligibility of the competitor as required in rule K3.1(a).
(c) The national authority shall promptly report a suspension of eligibility under rule 69.2(a) to the ISAF, and to the national authorities of the person or the owner of the boat suspended if they are not members of the suspending national authority.

69.3 Action by the ISAF

Upon receipt of a report required by rules 69.2(c) and K4.1, the ISAF shall inform all national authorities, which may also suspend eligibility for events held within their jurisdiction. The ISAF Executive Committee shall suspend the competitor's ISAF eligibility as required in rule K3.1(a) if the competitor's national authority does not do so.

SECTION D – APPEALS

70 RIGHT OF APPEAL AND REQUESTS FOR INTERPRETATIONS

70.1 Provided that the right of appeal has not been denied under rule 70.4, a protest committee's interpretation of a *rule* or its procedures, but not the facts in its decision, may be appealed to the national

authority of the venue by
(a) a boat or competitor that is a *party* to a hearing, or
(b) a race committee that is a *party* to a hearing, provided the protest committee is a jury.

70.2 A protest committee may request confirmation or correction of its decision.

70.3 A club or other organization affiliated to a national authority may request an interpretation of the *rules*, provided no *protest* that may be appealed is involved.

70.4 There shall be no appeal from the decisions of an international jury constituted in compliance with Appendix Q. Furthermore, if the notice of race and the sailing instructions so state, the right of appeal may be denied provided that
(a) it is essential to determine promptly the result of a race that will qualify a boat to compete in a later stage of an event or a subsequent event (a national authority may prescribe that its approval is required for such a procedure),
(b) a national authority so approves for a particular event open only to entrants under its own jurisdiction, or
(c) a national authority after consultation with the ISAF so approves for a particular event, provided the jury is constituted as required by Appendix Q, except that only two members of the jury need be International Judges.

70.5 Appeals and requests shall conform to Appendix F.

71 APPEAL DECISIONS

71.1 No *interested party* or member of the protest committee shall take any part in the discussion or decision on an appeal or a request for confirmation or correction.

71.2 The national authority may uphold, change or reverse a protest committee's decision, declare the *protest* invalid, or return the *protest* for a new hearing and decision by the same or a different protest committee.

71.3 When from the facts found by the protest committee the national authority decides that a boat that was a *party* to the hearing broke a *rule*, it shall penalize her, whether or not that boat or that *rule* was mentioned in the protest committee's decision.

71.4 The decision of the national authority shall be final. The national authority shall send its decision in writing to all *parties* to the hearing and the protest committee, who shall be bound by the decision.

PART 6 – ENTRY AND QUALIFICATION

75 ENTERING A RACE

75.1 To enter a race, a boat shall comply with the requirements of the organizing authority of the race. She shall be entered by
(a) a member of a club or other organization affiliated to a national authority,
(b) such a club or organization, or
(c) a member of a national authority.

75.2 Competitors shall comply with Appendix K, if applicable.

76 EXCLUSION OF BOATS OR COMPETITORS

76.1 The organizing authority or the race committee may reject or cancel the entry of a boat or exclude a competitor, subject to rule 76.2, provided it does so before the start of the first race and states the reason for doing so.

76.2 At world and continental championships no entry within stated quotas shall be rejected or cancelled without first obtaining the approval of the relevant international class association (or the Offshore Racing Council) or the ISAF.

77 IDENTIFICATION ON SAILS

A boat shall comply with the requirements of Appendix H governing class insignia, national letters and numbers on sails.

78 COMPLIANCE WITH CLASS RULES; CERTIFICATES

78.1 A boat's owner and any other person in charge shall ensure that the boat is maintained to comply with her class rules and that her measurement or rating certificate, if any, remains valid.

78.2 When a *rule* requires a certificate to be produced before a boat *races*, and it is not produced, the boat may *race* provided that the race committee receives a statement signed by the person in charge that the valid certificate exists and that it will be given to the race committee before the end of the event. If the certificate is not received in time, the boat's scores shall be removed from the event results.

78.3 When a measurer for an event concludes that a boat does not comply with her class rules, he shall report the matter in writing to the race committee, which shall protest the boat.

79 ADVERTISING
A boat and her crew shall comply with Appendix G.

80 RESCHEDULED RACES
When a race has been rescheduled, rule 36 applies and all boats entered in the original race shall be notified and, unless disqualified under rule 30.3, be entitled to sail the rescheduled race. New entries that meet the entry requirements of the original race may be accepted at the discretion of the race committee.

PART 7 - RACE ORGANIZATION

85 GOVERNING RULES
The organizing authority, race committee and protest committee shall be governed by the *rules* in the conduct and judging of races.

86 RULE CHANGES
86.1 A racing rule may not be changed unless permitted in the rule itself or as follows:
(a) Prescriptions of a national authority may change a racing rule, but not the Definitions; a rule in the Introduction; Sportsmanship and the Rules; Part 1, 2 or 7; rule 43.1, 43.2, 69, 70, 71, 75, 76.2 or 79; a rule of an appendix that changes one of these rules; or Appendix G, J, K, L or Q.
(b) Sailing instructions may change a racing rule by referring specifically to it and stating the change, but not rule 76.1, Appendix F, or a rule listed in rule 86.1(a).
(c) Class rules may change only rules 42, 49, 50, 51, 52, 53 and 54.

86.2 If a national authority so prescribes, these restrictions do not apply if rules are changed to develop or test proposed rules in local races. The national authority may prescribe that its approval is required for such changes.

87 ORGANIZING AUTHORITY; NOTICE OF RACE; COMMITTEE APPOINTMENTS
87.1 Organizing Authority
Races shall be organized by an organizing authority, which shall be
(a) the ISAF;
(b) a member national authority of the ISAF;
(c) a club or other organization affiliated to a national authority;
(d) a class association, either with the approval of a national authority or in conjunction with an affiliated club; or
(e) an unaffiliated body in conjunction with an affiliated club.

87.2 Notice of Race; Committee Appointments
The organizing authority shall publish a notice of race that conforms to rule M1, appoint a race committee and, when appropriate, appoint a jury.

88 RACE COMMITTEE; SAILING INSTRUCTIONS; SCORING
88.1 Race Committee
The race committee shall conduct races as directed by the organizing authority and as required by the *rules*.

88.2 Sailing Instructions
(a) The race committee shall publish written sailing instructions that conform to rule M2.
(b) The sailing instructions for an international event shall include, in English, the applicable prescriptions of the national authority.
(c) Changes to the sailing instructions shall be in writing and posted within the required time on the official notice board or, on the water, communicated to each boat before her warning signal. Oral changes may be given only on the water, and only if the procedure is stated in the sailing instructions.

88.3 Scoring
The race committee shall score a race or series as required in rule A1 and by the scoring system specified in the sailing instructions.

89 PROTEST COMMITTEE
A protest committee shall be
(a) a committee appointed by the race committee;
(b) a jury, which is separate from and independent of the race

committee; or
(c) an international jury meeting the requirements of Appendix Q. A national authority may prescribe that its approval is required for the appointment of international juries for races within its jurisdiction, except those of the ISAF.

APPENDIX A - SCORING

See rule 88.3.
A1 GENERAL SCORING RULES
These rules apply regardless of the scoring system in effect.

A1.1 Failure to Start or Finish
When the race committee scores a boat as failing to *start* or *finish* it need not protest her.

A1.2 Boat Retiring or Disqualified After Finishing
When a boat retires or is disqualified after *finishing*, each boat that *finished* after her shall be moved up one place.

A1.3 Scores Not Discardable
When a scoring system provides that one or more race scores are to be discarded in calculating a boat's series score, the score for disqualification under rule 2, or rule 42 when rule 67 applies, shall not be discarded.

A1.4 Unbroken Ties
(a) When boats are tied at the end of a race, the points for the place for which the boats have tied and for the place(s) immediately below shall be added together and divided equally. Boats tied for a prize shall share it or receive equal prizes.
(b) When boats have equal scores at the end of a series and a tie is unbroken by the scoring system, the scores shall remain unchanged in the final results. Boats tied for a prize shall share it or receive equal prizes.

A1.5 Numbering of Races
Races shall be numbered sequentially in the order of completion.

A1.6 A Boat's Starting Time
The time of a boat's starting signal shall be used as her starting time.

A1.7 Scores Removed from All or Part of a Series
When a boat is penalized by having her scores removed from the results of some or all races of a series, no changes shall be made in the race scores of other boats.

A2 SCORING SYSTEMS
The Bonus Point Scoring System and the Low Point Scoring System are the systems most often used. The bonus point system gives extra points for the first six places because it is harder to sail from fourth place into third, for example, than from fourteenth place into thirteenth. It is used for many class championships. The low point system is also suitable for championships, is better for small-fleet racing and is easier to use. Both systems are primarily designed for regattas but may be adapted for other series; see rule A5.

Either system may be made applicable by stating in the sailing instructions that the bonus point or low point system of Appendix A of the racing rules will apply and including the information required in rule A2.1.

A2.1 Number of Races and Series Scores
The number of races scheduled and the number required to constitute a series shall be stated in the sailing instructions. Each boat's series score will be the total of her race scores, discarding her worst score* except when prohibited in rule A1.3. The lowest series score wins.
* More than one score may be required to be discarded or all scores may be required to be counted; in either case the sailing instructions shall so state.

A2.2 Race Scores
Each boat *starting* and *finishing* in a race, and not thereafter retiring or being disqualified, will be scored points as follows:

Finishing place	Bonus point system	Low point system
First	0	1
Second	3	2
Third	5.7	3
Fourth	8	4
Fifth	10	5

Sixth	11.7	6
Seventh	13	7
Each place thereafter	Add 1 point	Add 1 point

All other boats will be scored points for the finishing place one more than the total number of boats entered in the series.

A2.3 Ties
When there is a tie in series points between two or more boats, the tie will be broken in favour of the boat with the most first places, or, if the tie remains, the most second places, or lower places if necessary, using only the scores for each boat that count for her series score. When a tie still remains, it will be broken in favour of the boat with the best score in the last race in which the tied boats *raced* and scored differently, using only the scores for each boat that count for her series score. For these calculations, if a boat has been awarded average points that do not correspond to a place, she shall be considered to have the place closest in points to the points awarded; if a boat has tied for a place, she shall be considered to have that place.

A3 ABBREVIATIONS FOR SCORING RECORDS
These abbreviations are recommended for recording the circumstances that determine a score:

DNC	Did not come to the starting area
DNS	Did not *start*
OCS	On the course side of the starting line and failed to comply with rule 29.1 or rule 30.1
DNF	Did not *finish*
RET	Retired after *finishing*
DSQ	Disqualified
DND	Disqualification not discardable because of rule A1.3
RDG	Redress given
ZPG	Z flag penalty given

A4 REDRESS
If under rule 64.2 the protest committee decides to change a boat's score, it should consider scoring her
(a) points equal to the average, to the nearest tenth of a point (0.05 to be rounded upward), of her points in all the races in the series except [her worst race and]* the race in question, or
(b) points equal to the average, to the nearest tenth of a point (0.05 to be rounded upward), of her points in all the races before the race in question, or
(c) points based on the position of the boat at the time of the incident that justified the redress.
* Delete these words when all scores count for series results, or adjust when more than one race is to be discarded.

A5 WHEN A SERIES IS NOT A REGATTA
In a regatta all boats are expected to compete in all races and the difference between the number of entrants and the number of starters is usually insignificant. However, in a longer series there may be a number of boats that compete in fewer races than others, in which case the following may be substituted for the second paragraph of rule A2.2:

Boats not so scored that came to the starting area will be scored points for the finishing place one more than the number of all boats that came to the starting area. Boats that did not come to the starting area will be scored points for the finishing place one more than the number of boats entered in the series.

APPENDIX G – ADVERTISING

See rule 79. This appendix shall not be changed by sailing instructions or prescriptions of national authorities. When governmental requirements conflict with parts of it, those requirements apply.

G1 DEFINITION OF ADVERTISING
For the purposes of this appendix, advertising is the name, logo, slogan, description, depiction, a variation or distortion thereof, or any other form of communication that promotes an organization, person, product, service, brand or idea so as to call attention to it or to persuade persons or organizations to buy, approve or otherwise support it.

G2 GENERAL
G2.1 Advertisements and anything advertised shall meet generally accepted moral and ethical standards.

G2.2 This appendix shall apply when *racing* and, in addition, unless otherwise stated in the notice of race, from 0700 on the first race day of a regatta until the expiry of the time limit for lodging *protests* following the last race of the regatta.

G2.3 An event shall be designated Category A, B or C in its notice of race and sailing instructions, but if not so designated it shall be Category A. However, at the world and continental championships of Olympic classes, Category B advertising shall be permitted on hulls and, for Olympic sailboard classes, on hulls and sails. After the notice of race has been published, the category shall not be changed within ninety days before the event without prior approval of the national authority of the organizing authority.

G2.4 A national authority, or a class or the Offshore Racing Council for its events, may prescribe *rules* for advertising that are more restrictive than those of a category. For a particular event, the notice of race and the sailing instructions may include *rules* for advertising that are more restrictive than those of the event's category.

G2.5 Advertisements on sails shall be clearly separated from national letters and sail numbers.

G2.6 When, after finding the facts, a protest committee decides that a boat or her crew has broken a rule of this appendix, it shall
(a) warn the boat that another breach of the rule will result in disqualification; or
(b) disqualify the boat in accordance with rule 64.1; or
(c) disqualify the boat from more than one race or from the series when it decides that the breach warrants a stronger penalty; or
(d) act under rule 69.1 when it decides that there may have been a gross breach.

G2.7 The ISAF, a national authority, a class association or the ORC may, for its events, subject to rule G5, designate the category and may require a fee for doing so.

G2.8 The ISAF or a national authority may, for its events, prescribe *rules* and require a fee for giving consent to individual boats for advertisements, provided that such consents do not conflict with, when relevant, class rules or the rules of the ORC.

G3 CATEGORY A
G3.1 Advertising on boats other than sailboards is permitted only as follows:
(a) The boat's class insignia may be displayed on her sails as required by Appendix H.
(b) One sailmaker's mark, which may include the name or mark of the sailcloth manufacturer and the pattern or model of the sail, may be displayed on both sides of any sail and shall fit within a 150 mm x 150 mm square. On sails other than spinnakers, no part of such mark shall be placed farther from the tack than the greater of 300 mm or 15% of the length of the foot.
(c) One builder's mark, which may include the name or mark of the designer, may be placed on the hull and one maker's mark may be displayed on spars and on each side of small equipment. Such marks shall fit within a 150 mm x 150 mm square.
(d) The boat's type name may be displayed on each side of her hull. Lettering shall not be higher than 1% or longer than 5% of the hull length of the boat, to a maximum of 100 mm or 700 mm respectively.
(e) Makers' marks may be displayed on clothing and equipment. Other advertising may be displayed on clothing and equipment ashore.
(f) The organizing authority of a sponsored event may permit or require the display of an advertisement of the event sponsor not larger than 0.27 m2 in the form of a flag, and/or of a decal or sticker attached to each side of the hull or to a dodger on each side of the boat. In addition, when a sponsor supplies all hulls and sails at no cost to the organizing authority or competitors, one advertisement not larger than 0.27 m2 may be displayed on each side of the mainsail. For an event of a class association or the ORC, such advertising requires approval by the class association or the ORC and, when it so prescribes, by the national authority concerned. Notice of such permission or requirement shall be included in the notice of race and the sailing instructions.

G3.2 Advertising on sailboards is permitted only as follows:
(a) The sailboard's class insignia may be displayed on her sail as required by Appendix H.
(b) One sailmaker's mark, which may include the name or mark of the sailcloth manufacturer and the pattern or model of the sail, may be displayed on both sides of the sail. No part of such mark shall be placed farther from the tack than 20% of the length of the foot of the sail, including the mast sleeve. The mark may also be displayed on the lower half of the part of the sail above the wishbone but no part of it

shall be farther than 500 mm from the clew.

(c) The sailboard's type or manufacturer's name or logo may be placed on the hull in two places and on the upper third of the part of the sail above the wishbone. One maker's mark may be displayed on spars, on each side of small equipment and on a competitor's clothing and harness.

(d) The organizing authority of a sponsored event may permit or require the display of an advertisement of the event sponsor on both sides of the sail between the sail numbers and the wishbone and on a bib worn by the competitor. For an event of a class association, such advertising requires approval by the class association and, when it so prescribes, by the national authority concerned. Notice of such permission or requirement shall be included in the notice of race and the sailing instructions.

G4　CATEGORY B

G4.1 A boat competing in a Category B event may display advertising only as permitted for Category A and by rule G4.2 (for boats other than sailboards) or rule G4.3 (for sailboards) and throughout that event shall not display advertising chosen by the boat of more than two organizations or persons. A Category B advertisement shall be either one or two of
(a) the name of an organization or person,
(b) a brand or product name, or
(c) a logo.

G4.2 Advertising on Boats Other than Sailboards

(a) The forward 25% of each side of the hull may display no more than two advertisements chosen by the ISAF, the national authority, the class association or the ORC, for its event; or by the organizing authority of the event when it wishes to display advertising of an event sponsor. When both the organizing authority and one of the other organizations wish to use the space, they shall each be entitled to half the length of the space on each side. The remaining length of the hull shall be free of any advertising except for that permitted in rule G3.1(c) and except that half that length may be used for advertising chosen by the boat. If advertising is not displayed on the sides of the hull, it may be displayed on each side of the cabin, the insides of the cockpit coamings or sidetanks, subject to the same length dimensions.

(b) Advertising chosen by the boat may be displayed on sails as follows:
(1) Advertising on spinnakers is without restriction except as provided in rules G2.5 and G4.
(2) On one other sail, only one advertisement may be carried at a time, and it may be on both sides of the sail. It shall be placed below the national letters and sail numbers and have a width no greater than two-thirds of the length of the foot of the sail and a height no greater than one-third of that width.

(c) Advertising chosen by the boat may be displayed on the mainmast and main boom, but both displays shall be limited to the name, brand or product name, or logo of one organization. The space within one-third of the length of the mast and two-thirds of the length of the boom may be used.

(d) In addition to the advertisements carried on the boat, advertisements limited to the organization(s) advertising on the boat and one or two additional organizations may be displayed on clothing and equipment worn by competitors.

G4.3 Advertising on Sailboards

(a) The forward 25% of the hull may display no more than two advertisements chosen by the ISAF, the national authority or the class association, for its event; or by the organizing authority of the event when it wishes to display advertising of an event sponsor. When both the organizing authority and one of the other organizations wish to use the space, they shall each be entitled to half the length of the space on each side. Advertising chosen by the competitor may be displayed within the remaining length of the hull.

(b) That part of the sail below the wishbone not used for Category A advertising may display advertising chosen by the competitor.

(c) In addition to the advertisements carried on the sailboard, advertisements limited to the organization(s) advertising on the sailboard and one or two additional organizations may be displayed on clothing and equipment worn by competitors.

G5 CATEGORY C ADVERTISING

G5.1　Approval of Advertising

Advertising for a Category C event (any event that permits advertising beyond Category B advertising) shall be
(a) approved by the national authority of the venue unless the event is an international event;
(b) approved by the International Sailing Federation (ISAF) when the event is an international event (i.e., an event open to entries other than those from the national authority of the venue).

G5.2 Advertising Fees

(a) National events: The national authority of the venue may require an advertising fee for approval of Category C advertising to be paid to it.
(b) International events: The ISAF will require an advertising fee for approval of Category C advertising, and will share the fee equally with the national authority of the venue.

G5.3 Approval Fees

The organizing authority of an event with cash or cashable prizes or appearance payments totalling more than US $10,000 or the equivalent may be required to pay an approval fee. For a national event the national authority of the venue may require such a fee to be paid to it. For an international event the ISAF will require such a fee to be paid to it.

G5.4 Rules for Category C advertising shall be stated in the notice of race and the sailing instructions

APPENDIX J – WEIGHING CLOTHING AND EQUIPMENT

See rule 43.1(b). This appendix shall not be changed by sailing instructions or prescriptions of national authorities.

J1 The items of a competitor's clothing and equipment to be weighed shall be arranged on a rack and thoroughly soaked by total immersion in water for one minute or longer if necessary for total saturation. After being soaked, the items shall be allowed to drain freely for one minute before they are weighed. Life-jackets shall be included, but not a hiking or trapeze harness or clothing worn only below the knee unless class rules require that it be included. The rack must allow the items to hang as they would hang from clothes hangers, so as to allow the water to drain freely. Hiking or trapeze harnesses shall be weighed separately and tested for positive buoyancy.

J2 During the weighing, pockets that have drainholes that cannot be closed shall be empty, but pockets or items of equipment that hold water shall be full.

J3 When a weight recorded exceeds the amount permitted, the competitor may twice rearrange the clothing and equipment on the rack and the measurer shall again soak and weigh it. If a lower weight is recorded that record shall be final.

J4 A competitor wearing a dry-suit may choose an alternative means of weighing:
(a)　the dry-suit and items of clothing and equipment that are worn outside the dry-suit shall be weighed as described above;
(b) clothing worn underneath the dry-suit shall be weighed as worn while *racing*, without draining; and
(c) the two weights shall be added together.

APPENDIX K – COMPETITORS' ISAF ELIGIBILITY

See rule 75.2. This appendix shall not be changed by sailing instructions or prescriptions of national authorities.

K1 ISAF ELIGIBILITY RULES

To be eligible to compete in an event listed in rule K2.1, a competitor shall
(a) be governed by the regulations and rules of the ISAF;
(b) be a member of a member national authority or one of its affiliated organizations. Such membership shall be established by the competitor
(1) being entered by the national authority of the country of which the competitor is a national or ordinarily a resident; or
(2) presenting a valid membership card or certificate, or other satisfactory evidence of identity and membership;
(c) not be under suspension of ISAF eligibility.

K2 EVENTS REQUIRING ISAF ELIGIBILITY

K2.1 ISAF eligibility is required for the following events:
(a) the sailing regatta of the Olympic Games;
(b) the sailing regattas of regional games recognized by the International Olympic Committee;
(c) events including 'ISAF' in their titles;
(d) world and continental championships of ISAF international classes and of the Offshore Racing Council; and
(e) any other event approved by the ISAF as a world championship and so stated in the notice of race and the sailing instructions.

K2.2　ISAF eligibility may be required for any other event when so stated in the notice of race and the sailing instructions with specific reference to this appendix.

K3 SUSPENSION OF ISAF ELIGIBILITY

K3.1 After proper inquiry by either the national authority of the competitor or the ISAF Executive Committee, a competitor's ISAF eligibility shall be promptly suspended with immediate effect, permanently or for a specified period of time
(a) for any suspension of eligibility in accordance with rule 69.2; or
(b) for breaking rule 5; or
(c) for competing, within the two years preceding the inquiry, in an event that the competitor knew or should have known was a prohibited event.

K3.2 A prohibited event is an event
(a) permitting or requiring advertising beyond that permitted for Category B under Appendix G that is not approved as required by that appendix;
(b) in which cash or cashable prizes and/or appearance payments totalling more than US $10,000 (or its equivalent) may be received by any one boat, that is not approved by the national authority of the venue or, for events conducted in more than one country, the ISAF; or
(c) that is described as a world championship, either in the title of the event or otherwise, and that is not approved by the ISAF. (ISAF approval is not required for world championships of ISAF international classes or of the Offshore Racing Council.)

K3.3 When an event described in rule K3.2 has been approved as required, that fact shall be stated in the notice of race and the sailing instructions.

K4 REPORTS; REVIEWS; NOTIFICATION; APPEALS

K4.1 When a national authority suspends a competitor's ISAF eligibility under rule K3.1, it shall promptly report the suspension and reasons therefor to the ISAF. The ISAF Executive Committee may revise or annul the suspension with immediate effect. The ISAF shall promptly report any suspension of a competitor's eligibility, or of its revision or annulment by the ISAF Executive Committee, to all national authorities, international class associations, the Offshore Racing Council and other ISAF affiliated organizations, which may also suspend eligibility for events held within their jurisdiction.

K4.2 A competitor whose suspension of ISAF eligibility has been either imposed by a national authority, or imposed or revised by the ISAF Executive Committee, shall be advised of the right to appeal to the ISAF Review Board and be provided with a copy of the Review Board Rules of Procedure.

K4.3 A national authority or the ISAF Executive Committee may ask for a review of its decision by the ISAF Review Board by complying with the Review Board Rules of Procedure.

K4.4 The Review Board Rules of Procedure shall govern all appeals and requests for review.

K4.5 Upon an appeal or request for review, the ISAF Review Board may confirm, revise or annul a suspension of eligibility, or require a hearing or rehearing by the suspending authority.

K4.6 Decisions of the Review Board are not subject to appeal.

K4.7 The ISAF shall promptly notify all national authorities, international class associations and the Offshore Racing Council of all Review Board decisions.

K5 REINSTATEMENT OF ISAF ELIGIBILITY

The ISAF Review Board may reinstate the ISAF eligibility of a competitor who
(a) applies for reinstatement;
(b) establishes substantial, changed circumstances justifying reinstatement; and
(c) has completed a minimum of three years of suspension.

APPENDIX L – BANNED SUBSTANCES AND BANNED METHODS

See rule 5. This appendix shall not be changed by sailing instructions or prescriptions of national authorities. When governmental requirements conflict with parts of it, those requirements apply.

INTRODUCTION

Doping is the taking or using by a competitor of a substance or a method banned by the ISAF. Doping is governed by rule 5, this appendix, and the ISAF *Medical Lists* (containing the official lists of doping classes and methods, medicines that may be taken, and laboratories accredited for doping control) and *Doping Control*

Procedures (the medical procedures leaflet). These publications, doping control forms and the ISAF schedule of penalties are available from the ISAF to national authorities and competitors on request.

L1 GENERAL

L1.1 No testing shall be initiated by the organizing authority of an event without the written authority of the ISAF or the national authority having jurisdiction over the event, except that at an event for an Olympic class it may be initiated by the national authority of the competitor to be tested.

L1.2 A competitor selected for testing shall not refuse to be tested and shall appear at a control centre when required by a sampling officer.

L2 INITIATION OF DOPING CONTROL

The ISAF or a national authority may at any time initiate medical testing to control doping within its own jurisdiction or for competitors under its jurisdiction. A sampling officer shall be appointed to administer or supervise the testing.

L3 SELECTION

L3.1 At an authorized event, the chairman of the protest committee shall select the finishing places of competitors to be tested on the day. This may be by means of a draw or by other means decided by the protest committee. When there is more than one competitor in each boat, any or all of them may be selected. The race committee shall give to the sampling officer the names of the competitors who *finished* in the selected places. When, for any reason, no boats have *finished* in the selected places, names may be selected by means of a draw. A competitor may be tested more than once during an event.

L3.2 When the ISAF or the national authority of a competitor under its jurisdiction initiates out-of-competition testing of a competitor, it shall test only after receiving written consent from the competitor. Any such testing shall take place within the period specified in the consent.

L4 PROCEDURE

L4.1 (a) The sampling officer or his representative shall inform a competitor by written notice, in confidence, that he or she has been selected for testing and is required to provide a urine sample at the time and place specified in the notice. The notice shall also specify the name of the sampling officer appointed for the event and of the designated laboratory to which specimens will be sent.
(b) The competitor shall acknowledge receipt of the notice, and the time of its delivery shall be recorded by the sampling officer or his representative.
(c) The competitor may be accompanied by one person of his or her choice.
(d) The *Medical Lists* and *Doping Control Procedures* shall be available to the competitor on request.
(e) A competitor who fails to appear at the appointed time and place or who refuses to provide a sample shall be removed, together with the boat in which he or she was sailing, from the event and all its results. The protest committee shall call a hearing in accordance with the rules of Part 5, Section B, to investigate the circumstances and report its findings to the ISAF or to the initiating national authority, and to the national authority of the competitor.

L4.2 The sampling officer and other persons involved in doping control shall act in accordance with *Doping Control Procedures* and shall explain all procedures for doping control to the competitor.

L4.3 The competitor shall be given a copy of the doping control form and shall sign it to acknowledge that he or she has been informed of the procedures.

L4.4 The competitor shall provide a postal or fax address at which, during the 60 days following the testing, he or she may be informed of the result of the test of sample B (rule L5).

L4.5 Failure by a competitor to acknowledge receipt of the notice (rule L4.1(b)), to sign the form (rule L4.3) or to provide an address will not be grounds for cancelling any penalty imposed for breaking rule 5.

L5 SAMPLING AND RESULTS

L5.1 The competitor shall provide a urine sample which will be divided into two samples, A and B, and sent to a designated laboratory.

L5.2 When sample A is negative, the sampling officer shall so inform the competitor immediately and no further action shall be taken.

L5.3 When sample A is positive
(a) the initiating authority shall so inform the competitor and his or her national authority immediately. No race results shall be changed at this stage; and
(b) the laboratory will proceed to test sample B. The competitor or his or her representative may be present at the testing.

L5.4 (a) When sample B is negative, the initiating authority shall so inform the competitor and his or her national authority, and no further action shall be taken.
(b) When no result has been obtained from sample B after 60 days from the date of the testing, the test shall be considered void and no further action shall be taken.

L5.5 When sample B is positive, the ISAF or the initiating national authority will inform the competitor in writing at the address provided (rule L4.4) and his or her national authority. The ISAF will inform the national authority having jurisdiction over the event.

L5.6 (a) Any positive result of a medical test shall be reported promptly by the initiating national authority to the ISAF.
(b) Any penalties imposed by the national authority for breaches of rule 5 or rule L1.2 shall be reported promptly to the ISAF.

L6 APPEAL PROCEDURE
L6.1 The competitor has 20 days from the date of the communication required in rule L5.5 to appeal to the International Medical Commission (IMC) of the ISAF. When after 20 days the competitor has not appealed, his or her national authority and that of the event will be notified of this fact.

L6.2 After the last day for submitting an appeal, penalties will be applied and the scores of the competitor and the boat in which he or she was sailing shall be removed from the results of the event.

L7 EXEMPTIONS
L7.1 A competitor may ask, only in writing, for prior approval from the IMC for the use of a banned substance or a banned method for special medical reasons. The reasons shall be stated and supported with medical evidence from a doctor.

L7.2 In offshore races of more than 50 nautical miles, the use during the race of any banned substance or banned procedure for emergency medical treatment shall be reported promptly to the protest committee, which shall inform the appropriate national authority and the ISAF. The IMC may retroactively approve such use.

L8 SUSPENSION OF ISAF ELIGIBILITY
L8.1 In addition to any penalty imposed under rule K3.1, a competitor who has broken rule 5 may have his or her ISAF eligibility suspended as provided in Appendix K.

L8.2 The competitor may appeal as provided in Appendix K.

L9 COMPETITOR'S EXPENSES
Any expenses incurred in connection with this appendix by a competitor shall be his or her responsibility.

DEFINITIONS

A term used as stated below is shown in italic type or, in preambles, in bold italic type.

Abandon A race that a race committee or protest committee *abandons* is void but may be resailed.

Clear Astern and Clear Ahead; Overlap One boat is *clear astern* of another when her hull and equipment in normal position are behind a line abeam from the aftermost point of the other boat's hull and equipment in normal position. The other boat is *clear ahead*. They *overlap* when neither is *clear astern* or when a boat between them *overlaps* both. These terms do not apply to boats on opposite *tacks* unless rule 18 applies.

Finish A boat *finishes* when any part of her hull, or crew or equipment in normal position, crosses the finishing line in the direction of the course from the last *mark* either for the first time or, if she takes a penalty, after complying with rule 31.2 or rule 44.2.

Interested Party A person who may gain or lose as a result of a protest committee's decision, or who has a close personal interest in the decision.

Keep Clear One boat *keeps clear* of another if the other can sail her course with no need to take avoiding action and, when the boats are *overlapped* on the same *tack*, if the *leeward* boat could change course without immediately making contact with the *windward* boat.

Leeward and Windward A boat's *leeward* side is the side that is or, when she is head to wind, was away from the wind. However, when sailing by the lee or directly downwind, her *leeward* side is the side on which her mainsail lies. The other side is her *windward* side. When two boats on the same *tack overlap*, the one on the *leeward* side of the other is the *leeward* boat. The other is the *windward* boat.

Mark An object the sailing instructions require a boat to pass on a specified side, excluding its anchor line and objects attached temporarily or accidentally.

Obstruction An object that a boat could not pass without changing course substantially, if she were sailing directly towards it and one of her hull lengths from it. An object that can be safely passed on only one side and an area so designated by the sailing instructions are also *obstructions*. However, a boat *racing* is not an *obstruction* to other boats unless they are required to *keep clear* of her or give her *room*.

Overlap See **Clear Astern and Clear Ahead; Overlap.**

Party A *party* to a hearing: a protestor; a protestee; a boat requesting redress; any other boat or a competitor liable to be penalized, including under rule 69.1; a race committee in a hearing under rule 62.1(a).

Postpone A *postponed* race is delayed before its scheduled start but may be started or *abandoned* later.

Proper Course A course a boat would sail to *finish* as soon as possible in the absence of the other boats referred to in the rule using the term. A boat has no *proper course* before her starting signal.

Protest An allegation by a boat, a race committee or a protest committee that a boat has broken a *rule*.

Racing A boat is *racing* from her preparatory signal until she *finishes* and clears the finishing line and *marks* or retires, or until the race committee signals a general recall, *postponement*, or *abandonment*.

Room The space a boat needs in the existing conditions while manoeuvring promptly in a seamanlike way.

Rule
   (a) The rules in this book, including the Definitions, Race Signals, Introduction, preambles, and the rules of an appendix when it applies, but not titles;
   (b) the prescriptions of a national authority, when they apply;
   (c) the sailing instructions;
   (d) the class rules except any that conflict with the rules in this book;
   (e) any other documents governing the event.

Start A boat *starts* when after her starting signal any part of her hull, crew or equipment first crosses the starting line and she has complied with rule 29.1 and rule 30.1 if it applies.

Tack, Starboard or Port A boat is on the *tack, starboard* or *port*, corresponding to her *windward* side.

Two-Length Zone The area around a *mark* or *obstruction* within a distance of two hull lengths of the boat nearer to it.

Windward See **Leeward and Windward.**

Also by Bryan Willis

Protests & Appeals gives clear and detailed guidance on protesting, defending a protest, requesting redress, reopening hearings, and appealing.

No-one likes protests, and the last place to learn is at a major championship. This guide shows you what to expect, details how to conduct yourself fairly but effectively, and give you the best chance of winning if you are in the right. It should be in the kitbag of every racing sailor.